OXFORD WORLD'S CLASSICS

—

FEDERICO GARCÍA LORCA

Selected Poems

—

Translated by
MARTIN SORRELL

With an Introduction and Notes by
D. GARETH WALTERS

UNIVERSITY PRESS

OXFORD
UNIVERSITY PRESS

Great Clarendon Street, Oxford ox2 6DP
Oxford University Press is a department of the University of Oxford.
It furthers the University's objective of excellence in research, scholarship,
and education by publishing worldwide in

Oxford New York

Auckland Cape Town Dar es Salaam Hong Kong Karachi
Kuala Lumpur Madrid Melbourne Mexico City Nairobi
New Delhi Shanghai Taipei Toronto

With offices in

Argentina Austria Brazil Chile Czech Republic France Greece
Guatemala Hungary Italy Japan Poland Portugal Singapore
South Korea Switzerland Thailand Turkey Ukraine Vietnam

Oxford is a registered trade mark of Oxford University Press
in the UK and in certain other countries

Published in the United States
by Oxford University Press Inc., New York

Spanish-language works by Federico García Lorca copyright © Herederos de Federico
García Lorca. Translations by Martin Sorrell copyright © Herederos de Federico García
Lorca and Martin Sorrell 2007
Introduction and Explanatory Notes © D. Gareth Walters 2007

The moral rights of the authors have been asserted
Database right Oxford University Press (maker)

First published as an Oxford World's Classics paperback 2007

British Library Cataloguing in Publication Data

Data available

Library of Congress Cataloging in Publication Data

García Lorca, Federico, 1898–1936.
[Poems. English. Selections]
Selected poems / Federico García Lorca; translated by Martin Sorrell; with an
introduction and notes by D. Gareth Walters.
p. cm. — (Oxford world's classics)
Includes bibliographical references and index.
ISBN-13: 978–0–19–280565–2 (alk. paper) 1. García Lorca, Federico, 1898—1936—
Translations into English. I. Sorrell, Martin. II. Title. III. Series.
PQ6613.A763A2 2007
861'.62—dc22
2007011367

Typeset by Cepha Imaging Private Ltd., Bangalore, India
Printed in Great Britain
on acid-free paper by
Clays Ltd, St Ives plc

ISBN 978-0-19-280565-2

1

OXFORD WORLD'S CLASSICS

SELECTED POEMS

FEDERICO GARCÍA LORCA was born into a landowning family in the vale of Granada in 1898. Eleven years later, his family moved to Granada itself, the scene of his formative artistic and intellectual contacts. After abandoning early plans for a musical career, Federico turned to literature; *Impressions and Landscapes* appeared in 1918. A year later began his long association with the Residencia de Estudiantes in Madrid. His many friends there included the poets Guillén and Alberti, the future film director Buñuel, and most importantly for Lorca, Salvador Dalí. Lorca's early plays and poems draw on aspects of Andalusian tradition, but always as part of a sophisticated language of highly personal expression. Dalí too encouraged him to make the exploration of his own unconscious a spur to more radical literary experiment. Thus when in 1928 his *Gypsy Ballads* achieved its outstanding popular success, Lorca had in a sense already moved beyond it. Partly in reaction to an unhappy homosexual love-affair he left Spain in 1929 to study at Columbia University. In the event his New York experiences sharpened his sense of crisis, confirming his sexual orientation and introducing new extremes of experiment into his writing: *Poet in New York* and the 'unperformable' drama, *The Public*. In 1931, the year following his return to Spain, the Second Republic was established. It brought Lorca a new commitment as director of the student theatre company 'La barraca', touring classic Spanish plays about the country. His literary projects of the early 1930s included new poetic ventures— *The Tamarit Divan*; the *Lament* for his bullfighter friend, Ignacio Sánchez Mejías—and, in *Blood Wedding*, *Yerma*, and *Doña Rosita the Spinster* a new kind of theatre: poetic, radical, questioning, but also accessible and popular. His success in this, his broad identification with progressive public causes, and his seemingly inexhaustible creativity made the Republican years a rewarding time for him. That was cut short when, in August 1936, a few weeks into the Civil War, and soon after finishing *The House of Bernarda Alba*, he was arrested and murdered by the Nationalist authorities in Granada.

MARTIN SORRELL is Emeritus Professor of Literary Translation at the University of Exeter, where he has spent most of his career teaching and researching French literature. For Oxford World's Classics he has translated volumes of verse by Rimbaud and Verlaine.

D. GARETH WALTERS is professor of Hispanic Studies at University of Wales, Swansea. He has written widely on Lorca and is the author of *An Introduction to Spanish Poetry: Spain and Spanish America* (2002).

OXFORD WORLD'S CLASSICS

*For over 100 years Oxford World's Classics have brought
readers closer to the world's great literature. Now with over 700
titles—from the 4,000-year-old myths of Mesopotamia to the
twentieth century's greatest novels—the series makes available
lesser-known as well as celebrated writing.*

*The pocket-sized hardbacks of the early years contained
introductions by Virginia Woolf, T. S. Eliot, Graham Greene,
and other literary figures which enriched the experience of reading.
Today the series is recognized for its fine scholarship and
reliability in texts that span world literature, drama and poetry,
religion, philosophy and politics. Each edition includes perceptive
commentary and essential background information to meet the
changing needs of readers.*

CONTENTS

Introduction   ix

Note on the Text and Translation   xxv

Select Bibliography   xxvii

A Chronology of Federico García Lorca   xxix

SELECTED POEMS
From *Book of Poems*

Canción otoñal 2	Autumn Song 3
Canción menor 6	Minor Song 7
Balada triste 8	Sad Ballad 9
Elegía 12	Elegy 13
Aire de nocturno 16	Nocturnal Air 17
Canción primaveral 18	Spring Song 19
Sueño 20	Dream 21
Balada de la placeta 22	Ballad of the Little Square 23
La balada del agua del mar 26	Seawater Ballad 27
Sueño 28	Dream 29
Otra canción 30	Another Song 31
El macho cabrío 32	The Billy Goat 33

From *Suites*

Canción con reflejo 38	Song with Reflection 39
Sésamo 40	Sesame 41
Canción bajo lágrimas 40	Song beneath Tears 41
Paisaje sin canción 42	Landscape without Song 43
Horizonte 42	Horizon 43
Pescadores 42	Fishermen 43
Delirio 44	Delirium 45
En el jardín de las toronjas de luna 44	In the Garden of Lunar Grapefruit 45

From *Poem of the Cante Jondo*

Paisaje 48	Landscape 49
La guitarra 48	The Guitar 49
El grito 50	The Shout 51
El silencio 52	The Silence 53

El paso de la Siguiriya 52	Dancing the *Siguiriya* 53
Después de pasar 52	After Passing By 53
Y después 54	And After 55
Tierra seca 54	Parched Land 55
Pueblo 56	Town 57
Puñal 56	Dagger 57
Encrucijada 58	Crossroads 59
¡Ay! 58	*Ay!* 59
Sorpresa 60	Surprise 61
La Soleá 60	The *Soleá* 61
Cueva 62	Cave 63
Encuentro 64	Meeting 65
Alba 64	Dawn 65
Arqueros 66	Bowmen 67
Noche 66	Night 67
Sevilla 68	Seville 69
Procesión 70	Procession 71
Paso 70	Float, Holy Week 71
Saeta 70	*Saeta* 71
Balcón 72	Balcony 73
Madrugada 72	Dawn 73

From *Songs*

Nocturnos de la ventana 76	Nocturnes at the Window 77
Canción tonta 80	Foolish Song 81
Canción de jinete 80	Horseman's Song 81
¡Es verdad! 82	It's true! 83
Verlaine 82	Verlaine 83
Baco 84	Bacchus 85
Juan Ramón Jiménez 84	Juan Ramón Jiménez 85
Venus 86	Venus 87
Debussy 86	Debussy 87
Narciso 88	Narcissus 89
Al oído de una muchacha 88	In a Girl's Ear 89
La luna asoma 90	The Moon Appears 91
Murió al amanecer 90	He Died at Dawn 91
Primer aniversario 92	First Anniversary 93
Segundo aniversario 92	Second Anniversary 93
Lucía Martínez 94	Lucía Martínez 95
La soltera en misa 94	The Spinster at Mass 95
Malestar y noche 94	Malaise and Night 95
Desposorio 96	Betrothal 97
Despedida 98	Parting 99
En el instituto y en la universidad 98	In the Institute and in the University 99

Madrigalillo 100   Light Madrigal 101

Preludio 100   Prelude 101

De otro modo 102   Another Way 103

Canción de noviembre y abril 102   Song of November and April 103

Canción del naranjo seco 104   Song of the Dry Orange Tree 105

From *Gypsy Ballads*

Romance de la luna, luna 106   Ballad of the Moon, the Moon 107

Romance sonámbulo 108   Dreamwalker Ballad 109

La monja gitana 112   The Gypsy Nun 113

Prendimiento de Antoñito el   Capture of Antoñito el
   Camborio en el camino   Camborio on the Seville
   de Sevilla 116   Road 117

Muerte de Antoñito el Camborio 118   Death of Antoñito el Camborio 119

Muerto de amor 122   Dead from Love 123

From *Poet in New York*

El rey de Harlem 126   The King of Harlem 127

Crucifixión 132   Crucifixion 133

Grito hacia Roma 136   Cry to Rome 137

Son de negros en Cuba 140   Blacks in Cuba, their *Son* 141

From *Earth and Moon*

Pequeño poema infinito 144   Little Infinite Poem 145

From *The Tamarit Divan*

Gacela IX Del amor maravilloso 146   Ghazal IX Of Marvellous Love 147

Casida V Del sueño al aire libre 146   Qasida V Of the Open-Air Dream 147

Casida VIII De la muchacha   Qasida VIII Of the Golden Girl 149
   dorada 148

Gacela del mercado matutino 150   Ghazal of the Morning
                         Marketplace 151

From *Six Galician Poems*

Romaxe de Nosa Señora   Romance of Our Lady of
   da Barca 152   the Boat 153

Canzón de cuna pra Rosalía   Cradle Song for Rosalía
   Castro, morta 152   Castro, Dead 153

Lament for Ignacio Sánchez Mejías 156

From *Sonnets of Dark Love*

El poeta habla por teléfono con
 el amor 170

The Poet Speaks to his Love on
 the Telephone 171

'¡Ay voz secreta del amor oscuro!' 170

'*Ay*, Secret Voice of Dark Love' 171

El amor duerme en el pecho
 del poeta 172

The Lover Asleep on the Poet's
 Breast 173

Noche del amor insomne 172

Night of Sleepless Love 173

Explanatory Notes   177

Index of Titles   185

Index of First Lines   189

INTRODUCTION

FEDERICO GARCÍA LORCA was born of a well-to-do family on 5 June 1898 in the village of Fuentevaqueros in the plain of Granada. From his father, a prosperous farmer and landowner, and from the family servants Lorca derived a love and knowledge of peasant life and rural lore that served to shape him as a writer. Before he was 4, he knew dozens of folk songs by heart, and such an early acquaintanceship with this material explains its ready assimilation into his poetry. The childlike quality of the verse and the ease with which Lorca could adopt a child's perspective may also derive from this exposure to the rich vein of Andalusian popular culture. In 1909, the family moved to Granada so that the educational needs of Federico and his brother and sister could be met. As schoolboy, student, and ultimately as a writer, Lorca was to base himself in Granada for the rest of his life. The spiritual kinship of the poet with the city, in particular with its Arabic heritage, is undoubted, as indeed is the association of Lorca with Andalusia as a whole. Important for his development as a writer, however, were study-visits he undertook as a student in 1916 and 1917 to other regions of Spain. Of crucial significance, too, for the development of his art was the period he spent living at the Residencia de Estudiantes in Madrid in the 1920s. The purpose of this institution, similar to an Oxbridge college, was to bring together the finest young talents of Spain and to help them blossom in an invigorating cultural and intellectual environment. Here Lorca formed close friendships with Salvador Dalí and Luis Buñuel. Stimulating in a different way was his experience as a student at Columbia University, New York, in 1929–30; it is nothing less than culture shock that is registered in a series of poems written during his stay in the city. Less inspiring, though certainly more enjoyable, was his South American tour of 1933–4. His fame was by now considerable in the Spanish-speaking world, and his trip coincided with successful productions of his plays. In 1931 the Education Ministry of the new government of the Second Republic had appointed him as director of a travelling theatre company, 'La barraca'. On his initiative, Spanish plays were performed all over the country, in squares, marketplaces, and barns. The effect on Lorca's own dramatic production was evident: the most powerful and popular of his plays were written in the few years between his practical theatrical experience and his death in 1936.[1]

In the turbulent days preceding the start of the Spanish Civil War in July of that year Lorca was in Madrid and confronted by a difficult choice. Should he remain in Madrid or return home to Granada as he normally did in the summer? Where would he be safer if hostilities were to break out? After some agonizing, he decided to go to Granada where he thought that he could rely on the protection of friends in the event of a Nationalist takeover. Indeed, within less than a month he was forced to seek refuge at the house of the family of a friend and fellow poet, Luis Rosales. They had connections with and thereby, it was hoped, influence upon the local Falangist party, a politico-military group charged with civic functions in the period following General Franco's revolt. Unfortunately, the Rosales were unable to save Lorca. Even while at their house, the Civil Governor issued an order for his arrest. He was detained on 16 August and executed by firing squad three days later along with a small group of his fellow citizens on a hillside above the town.

The subject of Lorca's death was for many years something of a forbidden topic. The outcry that followed, outside Spain as much as inside it, given the international impact of the Civil War and the fame that his works immediately achieved, proved embarrassing for the representatives of the Franco regime. Only since the 1970s have the facts about Lorca's death and the true motives been made public. Rumours that his death was prompted by purely personal factors, such as jealousy arising from a homosexual liaison, were useful in deflecting attention away from the political dimension.[2] Yet Lorca was not political in a committed partisan way, although his instincts were decidedly liberal and democratic in nature and he had aligned himself with left-wing values in the years preceding the start of the Civil War. Moreover, from his youth he had offended the Granada bourgeoisie by associating with some of the more flamboyant and arty types of the city. His homosexuality, although not blatant, further outraged the conservative-minded citizens. The seeds of resentment were further watered in an interview Lorca gave in

[1] See Federico García Lorca, *Four Major Plays*, trans. John Edmunds (Oxford: Oxford University Press, 1997).

[2] See Jean-Louis Schonberg, *Federico García Lorca: L'Homme-L'Œuvre* (Paris: Plon, 1956) and a summary of Schonberg's thesis in Ian Gibson, *The Death of Lorca* (London: Paladin, 1974), 154–7.

the last year of his life, in which he expressed the view that the capture of the Moorish kingdom of Granada by the Catholic Monarchs, Ferdinand and Isabella, was a 'disastrous event'.[3]

The popularity of Lorca's work is due in part to the circumstances of his death and the mystery in which it was shrouded. Yet he is also perceived, especially by readers in the English-speaking world, as the epitome of what it is to be a Spanish writer. Images of guitars, moons, violence, and passion occur with just enough regularity to justify the label. Such a view may not be a distortion, but it is certainly a simplification, and an awareness of Lorca's first faltering steps as a poet serves to caution against any view of him as a facile or even a 'natural' poet. In 1917–18, around the age of 20, he wrote several thousand lines of poetry; in terms of sheer productivity this was the most prolific period of his poetic career. Even though the poet and his brother Francisco had numbered the poems in readiness for publication, however, little of this vast output was to appear with the poet's blessing. This was a wise decision for there is little of genius or even charm in these earnest, inflated compositions for all their exuberance and pretension. Their publication in a popular paperback edition in 1994, as opposed to a more specialist one, was therefore questionable: a reader new to the poet could hardly recognize in this large volume the portents of talent or the hallmarks of style, and could indeed be dissuaded from reading other works of his. The true worth of the poetic juvenilia was that of a necessary apprenticeship. They afforded a space and opportunity for learning through the very act of writing poetry, acquiring the negative but crucial value of an exorcism. That Lorca could within five years be producing exquisite and disturbing miniatures speaks volumes for his capacity for self-analysis and self-criticism. His ambition was channelled ruthlessly into a practical awareness of what it took to become a poet.

Book of Poems

Before embarking on his poetic adventure Lorca seemed destined for a career in music. A highly talented pianist and a budding composer,

---

[3] 'An admirable civilization, and a poetry, architecture, and sensitivity unique in the world—all were lost, to give way to an impoverished, cowed city, a "miser's paradise" where the worst middle class in Spain today is busy stirring things up.' Cited in Ian Gibson, *Federico García Lorca* (London: Faber and Faber, 1989), 439.

he had hoped to pursue his musical studies in Paris. Parental oppo-
sition and the death of his music teacher, Antonio Segura, combined
to stifle this aspiration. In an autobiographical note written during
his period in New York in 1929–30 he relates his decision to become
a poet to thwarted musical ambitions: 'As his parents did not allow
him to go to Paris to continue with his initial studies and as his music
teacher died, García Lorca turned his (dramatic) pathetic creative
urges towards poetry.'[4] Such a clear-cut statement of cause and effect
may be an exaggeration, a simplified retrospective gloss. In any case
Lorca did not abandon music. His friendship with Manuel de Falla,
his organization jointly with Falla of a *cante jondo* festival—designed
to reinvigorate traditional Andalusian folk music (literally 'deep song'),
which had suffered from trivialization at the hands of café perform-
ers—and his imaginative arrangements of Spanish folk songs for
voice and piano all provide evidence of the continuing significance of
music in his work as well as in his life.[5]

In Lorca's earliest poetry there is, though, an overdependence
upon musical analogies as though the musician was only letting
go with reluctance. He utilizes composers' names as a shorthand or
code for a desired emotion and employs technical terms such as
tempo markings, key signatures, and symphonic or sonata movement
names. Such a heavy-handed manner is characteristic of the poetic
juvenilia, with their ready recourse to enumeration and anaphora,
liberally sprinkled with exclamation and interrogation marks.
It is not surprising then that only a handful of the 155 poems that
appear in the edition of the juvenilia should have found their
way into print. Of a different level of achievement altogether is
Book of Poems, a collection of sixty-eight poems written between
1918 and 1920. Uneven though it may be in quality, it offers a
distinctive glimpse into the making of a poet. If the unpublished
juvenilia are a place for the disposal of an inauthentic lyric voice,
then the first publication in verse constitutes a site for the gradual

---

[4] 'Como sus padres no permitieron que se trasladase a París para continuar con sus
estudios iniciales, y su maestro de música murió, García Lorca dirigió su (dramático)
patético afán creativo a la poesía.' *Obras completas*, ed. Arturo del Hoyo, 13th edn. (Madrid:
Aguilar, 1967), 1698.

[5] See my article 'Parallel trajectories in the careers of Falla and Lorca', in Federico
Bonaddio and Xon de Ros (eds.), *Crossing Fields in Modern Spanish Culture* (Oxford:
Legenda, European Humanities Research Centre, 2003), 92–102.

and painful acquisition of identity and aspiration. The collection is rich in a creative tension that is symptomatic of a learning curve. Such strains and conflicts can be found both in individual poems and between poems. The 'Elegy' (p. 13) is lexically overripe but it is also concentrated in its vision: the short-winded accumulation of the unpublished poetry yields to an arresting precision of imagery through the interplay of the sexual and the maternal, of Christianity and paganism. The pathetic fallacy in the poems entitled 'Songs' from the early part of the collection is countered by the edgy lyricism in the form of fragmentary dialogue and subterranean narrative in the poems entitled 'Ballads'. Strategically placed at the end of *Book of Poems* are a dozen or so poems that serve to embody discovery and adventure. Their unease is reminiscent of an idea in Shaw's *Major Barbara*: 'You have found something. At first that feels as if you have lost something.' The significantly named 'Another Song' (p. 31) marks such a coincidence of loss and gain, while 'Dream' (p. 29) and 'The Billy Goat' (p. 33), sexually dark and ambivalent, daringly stake out the new territory. Yet 'The Billy Goat' is perhaps less important for what it tells us about Lorca's sexuality in 1919 when it is supposed his homosexual inclination was not yet evident— and more significant as an indicator of a poetic crisis. In this respect, the roughness and aggression of the poem—the blunt terminology, the visceral phrasing—are if not a metaphor, then a working out (in both senses of the term) of expressive problems. It is a poetry that wears on its sleeve the excitement attendant upon the very making of the poem as a new kind of aesthetic experience, where 'light is a hurricane'.

Suites

What writing *Book of Poems* may have taught Lorca, among other things, was the art of minimalism. He was not especially interested in the various ephemeral Hispanic avant-garde poetic movements that were in vogue around 1920, but in the two years prior to the publication of *Book of Poems* his artistic horizons had widened with his entry into the Residencia de Estudiantes. The quest for a new and fresh poetic was manifested initially in the poems that came to comprise his *Suites*. The title suggests two musical models: the characteristic eighteenth-century composition of a kind much employed by

Bach and Handel, containing a whole range of dance forms, and an earlier type in the form of theme and variations, or what Spanish instrumental composers of the sixteenth century labelled 'diferencias'. More significant than the musical inspiration for the poetic form is the fastidiousness and precision of diction, a far remove from the verbosity of the unpublished poems and some compositions of *Book of Poems*. Yet the poem entitled 'Song with Reflection' (p. 39) reveals not just the effect of purgation, for its minimalism is not a matter of style—of an optional vehicle of presentation—but a mode of dramatization that is integral to the poem. While a reference to the poet's heart might have spawned an emotional rhapsody in the earliest poetry, here the term prompts distancing and a gentle irony. What we have are faint impressions and evasions in the unanswered questions and elisions. Such an abbreviated and truncated piece can hardly be *expressive* of anything, let alone of personal emotions, such is its incompleteness, its gaps. The 'lost language' in a sense says it all: it is a cavernous composition with the resonance of echo. What its unremitting suggestiveness approximates to are intimations of a relationship, as faceless as it is wordless, and as fleeting and insubstantial as the reflection of its title. It is a salutary reminder that poems work on the basis of what comes out of them rather than what certainly or allegedly goes into them.

Poem of the Cante Jondo

The *cante jondo* festival that Lorca organized in collaboration with Manuel de Falla and the businessman Miguel Cerón Rubio in 1922 inspired the *Poem of the Cante Jondo*, a work that could be considered as the greatest set of suites, although not named as such. In *cante jondo* Lorca discovered a depth and authenticity of folklore that readily translated into a form of poetry that he favoured in the early 1920s. Earlier poets, such as Manuel Machado, exploited the 'deep song' of the gypsies and their culture to supply word-pictures that veered between photographic realism and unintentional caricature. Lorca avoided the clichés of such a heady art and lifestyle. The key to his imagining of this ancient Andalusian song is evocation; in a lecture given to the Arts Club in Granada some months before the festival took place he described in suggestively poetic terms the character of this art: 'It is a song without landscape and therefore concentrated in itself and terrible amid the shadow.'[6] Such a mode of description is indicative of Lorca's approach in this collection. He is more concerned to assimilate rather than duplicate the detail of *cante jondo*: he may occasionally adopt its lexical mannerisms but he never quotes verbatim, however much he values its mystery. Instead he seeks an equivalence of effect.

One of the characteristics of flamenco song is voice modulation, enhanced by the use of the melisma, a decorative treatment of melody. The elaboration of the refrain in the final lines of '*Ay!*' (p. 59) is a case in point. It conveys that kind of stillness that we might be tempted to label unworldly until we realize that it is the very embodiment of world. It is a stillness where silence resounds—the presence of silence is no less significant in Lorca's plays—and where the shadow is the picture. In this scene of emptiness the plea for release and abandonment is formulated in a line of almost painful intensity so emphatically is it spelled out, syllable by syllable: 'I've told you to leave me.' Even in 'The Guitar' (p. 49) that celebrates the unique sound world of flamenco it is the echo or the memory of song that resonates. The repeated similes shadow a fading sound and register the immensity of the disappearing acoustic, such is their sheer sense of size and space. 'like water, | like wind | over snow'.

Commentators have sought to emphasize the tragic and dramatic aspects of the *cante jondo* poems, by reference both to Lorca's life and other works of his. Yet it is performance that the book's subdivisions highlight, by evoking the characteristic flamenco genres. The form of the suite enables an integration that mimics what actually happens in *cante jondo*: the guitar preceding the voice, the song that opens with an ornate cry of pain, the sequences in time. The compositions that form the 'Poem of the *Saeta*' are an impression of Holy Week in Seville. They acknowledge the solemnity of the occasion without being serious, and although they embody mystery insofar as they enunciate the dark and the remote, they also have an uncertain, elusive quality that is not so much spiritual as playful. Lorca puns on the word *saeta*, stubbornly refusing to take it purely as a metaphor—the songs as arrows of lamentation—and, denying the title of the section its true significance, thereby converts the *saeta* singers into bowmen,

---

[6] 'Es un canto sin paisaje, y por tanto, concentrado en sí mismo y terrible en medio de la sombra'. *Obras completas*, 47.

even establishing a witty link with the mythological archer, Cupid. In a further twist, the blind bowmen are connected to the hooded penitents of the brotherhoods that participate in the Good Friday processions. What such traits suggest is that in *Poem of the Cante Jondo* Lorca learnt how to make a 'bigger' work than hitherto. He betrays a capacity for thinking in larger structures: he attains a conception of a macro-poem made up of a number of smaller poems.

Songs

Such an accomplishment was to be consolidated in *Songs*, a work that occupied the poet mainly between 1921 and 1924 and which can be considered the culmination of his early poetry. In particular, it is in this collection that the functioning of the lyric presence, that had been tenaciously confronted in *Book of Poems* and controlled in *Poem of the Cante Jondo*, would be supremely refined. This presence is complex: the child's view of the world, open-eyed and undiscriminating, alternates with adolescent anxieties and with adult explanations or, just as often, evasions. In 'Nocturnes at the Window' (p. 77) there is an impulse prompted by the fascination of seeing, embodied in the magnetism of the moon, associated, as so often in Lorca's work, with fateful striving. In the lunge towards new experiences, the recklessness of the child-speaker is obvious. For if the danger is unwelcome, it is the price to be paid for the pleasure of finding out: the window through which the child puts his head to savour the smells of the night becomes a guillotine. The concluding poem in 'Nocturnes' (p. 79) suggests the confusion attendant upon discovery: the childlike visualization of a funeral serves as a cover for the fright of a lost innocence.

Many poems in *Songs* have as their site the boundary between childhood and adolescence; in 'Foolish Song' (p. 81) the yearning to move into the next stage of life is successfully countered by an instinctive regression. The incorporation of dialogue into the slightest of lyrics, as here, is one of the poet's touches of genius. Like others, this poem is a blend of neo-classical purity and pseudo-folkloric simplicity. In Lorca's hands, however, such a fusion yields unease, as in the edgy, truncated poems that either provide unhappy versions of the rites of courtship (pp. 89, 99, 101) or else brutally deconstruct them (pp. 95, 97). It is tempting to interpret such negative rationalizations of amatory aspiration and encounter as indications of the poet's homosexuality, and it is no great task to engage in what would be therefore warranted as appropriate decoding. This kind of approach—reductive as it is—often has the sole effect of telling us what we want to find out about the poet because we already know it. In any case it does not do justice to the complexity of the issue. In the sequence beginning with 'Verlaine' (p. 83) the layers of concealment prevail over any imperative of revelation. 'Bacchus' (p. 85) hints at a revulsion with the feminine through panic provoked by the fig-tree, a traditional female symbol. We could envisage a brief narrative whereby the speaker is approached by a female figure who seeks an intimate embrace only for him to recoil before her. In 'Venus' (p. 87) the 'shell of the bed' brings to mind the well-known Botticelli painting of the birth of Venus except that in Lorca's version Venus sinks into the sea rather than rises out of it—a blunt de-mythification that commemorates the death of woman as erotic objective. By contrast the vision of likeness through the reflection of the self—a same-sex attraction—in 'Narcissus' (p. 89) provokes fascination and desire—a process again realized by means of a child–mother dialogue. Yet the last word belongs to the poet who comments on what has occurred and asserts his right not to communicate: 'I understood. But I shan't explain.' One could not imagine a more robust disassociation from the conventional notion of poetry as the expression of emotion.

There are, admittedly, poems of the most sonorous and evocative character, such as 'Horseman's Song' (p. 81), where the rhythmic form magically shadows the doom-laden journey towards an unattainable Córdoba, or 'Song of the Dry Orange Tree' (p. 105) whose emotional unburdening and anguished articulation is more in keeping with the speech of the female figures of the late tragedies—the Mother in *Blood Wedding*, Yerma in the play of the same name, Adela in *The House of Bernarda Alba*—than the poetry of the early 1920s. Entirely different in nature is 'Parting' (p. 99). It is reminiscent of some of the quieter pieces in *Poem of the Cante Jondo*. There is a poise about the placing of the figures, each to his function: the poet on the balcony, the child eating oranges, the reaper in the fields. This spatial harmony is complemented by the uncluttered sentence-structure, simply and finely shaped. Here the restless gaze of the child in 'Nocturnes at the Window' is replaced by the weary contemplation of the adult, albeit languorous rather than dejected.

Gypsy Ballads

Yet perhaps the most emotive incorporation of the child in Lorca's poetry does not occur in *Songs* but in the opening poem, 'Ballad of the Moon, the Moon' (p. 107), of the next published collection, *Gypsy Ballads*. The uncanny fantasy of the moon who comes to the forge in order to abduct a child reveals Lorca at his most characteristically creative. In a lecture recital on the *Ballads* he observed that this was an invented myth: the moon as deadly ballerina. Yet part of its troubling attraction resides in its capacity to prod the reader into acknowledging other myths, as in the unconscious allusion to fragments of tales such as the 'Erlkönig' of Germanic legend. Above all, there is the conscious evocation of the world of the Spanish ballad—the *romance*—a traditional form that attracted 'learned' poets from the sixteenth century onwards. The sing-song repetition, both entranced and threatening in this ballad about the moon, the lavish detail, the sudden spurts of narrative energy, are all celebrated in this collection. The book's fame inspired all kinds of overall interpretation, including some by the poet himself, who felt obliged to defend it both against the contempt of his fellow artists, Dalí and Buñuel, who felt it to be a betrayal of the surrealist agenda, and against the misconceptions of those who believed the author himself to be a gypsy, such was its insight into their lives and culture. Yet as much as about Granada, or gypsies, or the 'pena negra' (dark grief)—the title of one of the poems—this book of ballads could be said to be about the ballad itself. It is a showcase of styles and mannerisms, from the virtuosity of its rhythmic variety to its tellingly authentic employment of one of the traits of the older form of the genre, the *romance viejo*: 'fragmentism', that is the practice of presenting the material of poems in the form of successive tableaux without connecting threads, and frequently having abrupt endings where the reader is deprived of a knowledge of the outcome.

It is one of the best known of all Lorca's poems that betrays this trait, the 'Dreamwalker Ballad' (p. 109). The subject of innumerable interpretations, variously ingenious and preposterous, it none the less refuses to yield a clear narrative.[7] Lorca himself observed that although

---

[7] 'Events become ambiguous, the poem remains open-ended, and linear, anecdotal interpretations are subsequently confounded.' Federico Bonaddio, 'Lorca's "Romance sonámbulo": The Desirability of Non-Disclosure', *Bulletin of Hispanic Studies*, 72 (1995), 385–401 (at 389).

it had 'a great sense of anecdote, nobody knows what happens, not even me'. The poem's fragmentism resides in the isolation of scenes, caused by the absence of explanatory connections, which compels us to fill the gaps by hazarding supposed causes and effects. Yet this should not be viewed as the product of a riddle-producer. The poem is imbued with a dream-like quality which has been an encouragement for the psycho-analytic school of critics, especially eager to press the case for Lorca as a man of his times, as one of a group of poets who were, it is to be pre-sumed, 'decisively influenced by the knowledge represented by Freud and Jung'.[8] But the features of this poem that linger in the mind and haunt the memory are likely to be uniquely poetic: from the haunting opening refrain—as good an example of the necessary inexplicable quality of poetry as one could imagine—to the heady confusion of dia-logue, description, and narrative of the poem's non-conclusion.

The sense of delight that comes from reading—or hearing—such a poem is repeated elsewhere in *Gypsy Ballads*. Commentators who extract anguished and tragic messages or statements from the work are in danger of forgetting the form in which such supposed portentous utterances are cast. Moreover, these poems betray a lightness of touch, an imaginative verve and even touches of humour. Such are the two ballads about Antoñito el Camborio (pp. 117–21), in real life a gypsy layabout who met an ignoble death after drinking too much, but ele-vated by Lorca into a delightfully cult, if not camp, figure: a pretty young man, carefree and swaggering, whose meek submission to the officers of the Civil Guard is redeemed in the duel with his cousins, the description of his balletic grace in the struggle recalling the metaphors drawn from the art of bullfighting in the previous poem. Lorca observes, tongue in cheek, that Antoñito was one of the purest heroes of the book as he was the only one to call him by name at the moment of his death: 'Oh, Federico García | call the Civil Guard!'

Poet in New York

In the summer of 1929 Lorca embarked from Southampton on the SS *Olympic* for New York. He was passing through a period of

---

[8] 'decisivamente influida por la ciencia representada por Freud y Jung'. J. M. Aguirre, 'El sonambulismo de Federico García Lorca', *Bulletin of Hispanic Studies*, 44 (1967), 267–85 (at 268).

depression, partly at least as a result of an amatory disappointment: the sculptor Emilio Aladrén, with whom he was infatuated, was starting to become interested in the girl who was to become his wife. The poet's stay in New York is commonly regarded as a miserable experience, one which Lorca translated into the anguished and difficult compositions published posthumously as *Poet in New York*. This is perhaps an oversimplification produced by the need to square the life with the work; in reality, Lorca was well received, even fêted, and relished the music of the blacks, whom he compared to the gypsies of his native Andalusia. He did, however, feel alienated from the life and, more especially, the lifestyle of New York, although only he could be blamed for this. He made little effort to learn English and displayed an instinctive antipathy to Anglo-Saxon culture and religion: his letters home are evidence of a closed mind. Not even a month in the country at the Vermont home of the parents of Philip Cummings, a young American student whom Lorca had met at the Residencia de Estudiantes the previous year, sufficed to relieve his depression. A poem he wrote when stopping off at Cuba on the way home is a joyous cry of relief: his verse seems to sing and dance again (p. 141).

Out of the New York experience Lorca made a poetry that is perhaps less individually distinctive than some of his previous work. The notion of the city as a dehumanizing environment, his revulsion at the multitudes who crowded Coney beach on holiday, and his lyrical disassociation from what he considered disagreeable or unacceptable, are hallmarks of a kind of artistic sensibility provocatively outlined by John Carey in *The Intellectuals and the Masses*. Lorca's natural sympathy for the underdog and his sense of decency coexist with an aristocratic, even elitist, air. Such a fusion leads to a poetry of bold strokes, even of simplicities. To extrapolate ideas from *Poet in New York* and write about them as if they were the poem is poor critical practice and an unjust tool of assessment: Lorca is a poet, not an essayist, to be judged on the poetic assimilation and integration of ideas not on their value in themselves. He fantasizes about how nature will one day wreak retribution on the metropolis, he denounces the world of money and numbers, and he manufactures a rhetoric of revolt. The vivacity of the imagination and the verve of the spoken voice (for many of the New York poems are splendid recitation pieces, as Lorca himself realized) are such that we overlook the embarrassingly rough-edged ideology. None the less, occasional outbursts make for uncomfortable reading: the liberating desire to 'beat | the little trembling Jewish women full of bubbles' would have been the subject of greater scandal in a poet for whom there might be less obvious affection, such as T. S. Eliot. That there are profoundly self-searching compositions in the collection touching on matters of religious speculation and sexual identity is not in doubt. Their tortuous probing, allied to a deployment of imagery that approximates to that of the surrealists, makes for difficult reading, though it has proved a rich seam for scholars. At his best, in a poem such as 'Cry to Rome' (p. 137), almost certainly inspired by the signing of the Lateran treaties between Mussolini and Pius XI in February 1929, the controlled imagery and rhetoric produces a stunning protest poem, a rare piece of poetic demagoguery whose incitements—denunciation and exhortation—have the ring of poetic truth.

The Tamarit Divan

In the last six years of his life Lorca wrote comparatively little poetry. His main focus of attention in this period was the stage, partly as a result of his appointment as the director of 'La barraca'. Indeed some of the finest poetry in these years is to be found in the three tragedies, not only in the set-piece poems, frequently in the guise of songs, but also in the sharp melodies of dialogue. He also returned to the kind of poetry he wrote in the early 1920s. The poems that appear in *The Tamarit Divan* are brief and evocative—an attempt to conjure up the delicate and exotic world of Arabic poetry. Though there are few formal connections between the ghazals and qasidas and the Arab genres from which this terminology derives, Lorca again succeeds— as he had with *Poem of the Cante Jondo*—in assimilating the essence and the flavour of such poetry. It is hardly surprising that a poetic imagination as attuned to place and history as Lorca's, growing up in the last stronghold of Moorish Spain, surrounded by sumptuous and sensuous palaces, gardens, and fountains, should react so creatively to a culture that he was to compare, favourably and provocatively, to that of the Christians who conquered Granada in 1492.

Six Galician Poems

The *Six Galician Poems* testify to an affection for Galicia that dated from a visit to the region as a student at the University of Granada and was reinforced by a more recent one with his theatre company. Lorca was also on friendly terms with a number of Galician writers and knew the literature of the region well. One of the poems (p. 153) pays homage to the greatest of the region's poets, Rosalía de Castro, and it also harks back to the medieval Galician-Portuguese lyric in its utilization of the dawn-song, albeit with an unusual macabre edge.

Lament for Ignacio Sánchez Mejías

The most ambitious poem of Lorca's last years is what could be termed an occasional piece. It is perhaps indicative of the way in which his allegiance was changing from poetry to drama that it should have taken a specific event to prompt him to such a work. In October 1934 the bullfighter Ignacio Sánchez Mejías, a friend of the poet, died as a result of a goring by a bull in a *corrida* in Manzanares, a small town south of Madrid. Mejías had retired from the ring some years earlier and his surprising return was foolhardy: now in his forties, he was overweight and had lost his former agility. His friendship with Lorca went back a number of years as, unusually for a bullfighter, albeit the son of a distinguished doctor, he had literary pretensions and talent, notably as a dramatist. The poem that Lorca wrote in his memory (p. 157) is a lament rather than an elegy—the Spanish term *llanto* of its title derives from the Latin *planctus* with its association of weeping. Both the title and passages in the poem's second part recall the most celebrated poem of this type in Spanish literature—the fifteenth-century 'Coplas por la muerte de su padre' ('Verses upon the Death of His Father') by Jorge Manrique. The best-known section of the poem is the opening with its endlessly repeated refrain 'At five in the afternoon'. From the poem we would imagine this to be the time of Mejías's death, but Lorca had obtained the phrase from a newspaper headline that employed the very same words in a reference to the start of the funeral procession some days later. To say it is a refrain is an understatement; it rings through the opening section of the poem like a maddening bell behind which the snatches of narrative are assembled. It is a virtuouso performance comparable to the *Gypsy Ballads*. There are subtle touches of technical wizardry: the changes of tense, the shift from metaphor to simile, above all, the elaboration of the refrain at strategic points like hammer blows resounding above the monotonous tolling.

The sensation of horror and the sense of anger that are traditionally part of the *planctus* yield in the later part of the poem to a resigned sorrow culminating in the tribute to the dead man and the implied consolation of his memory. The calmer vision prompts some of Lorca's most harmonious lines, the opening stanzas of the final section with their simple syntactical repetitions and the haunting evocation of autumn appropriately linger in the memory. Cultivated and brilliant though he may have been, Mejías was dignified beyond his significance by this noble threnody, converted into an Andalusian hero as Antoñito el Camborio had been years earlier.

Sonnets

In the last months of his life Lorca was planning a book of sonnets. This was not a form he had cultivated widely, but when he composed a group of eleven love sonnets at the end of 1935 it came at a moment when the form was enjoying something of a revival. Most of these poems were unpublished until the 1980s, as indeed had been the *Suites*. In the case of the sonnets, however, the delay in publication excited more interest. The title by which they are now known— *Sonnets of Dark Love*—was not one that appeared in the manuscript, but it has arisen because Lorca supposedly referred to them as such to friends. Inspired by Lorca's love for Rafael Rodríguez Rapún, a young engineering student with whom he had fallen in love in 1933, the term 'dark' is commonly taken as being synonymous with 'homosexual'. This is a reasonable deduction but Andrew Anderson is right to point out that the term has other connotations, 'most of them equally or more relevant to the appreciation of the sonnets as self-sufficient literary texts'. This scholar also perceptively observes that they are about 'the tormented *experience* of love, passion and suffering, and only secondarily about the dynamics of being in a love affair'.[9] There is little by way of specificity in the group of sonnets: indeed on only one occasion is the sexual identity of the object of love made explicit.

The reception of Lorca's work—his poetry in particular—has suffered from two successive distortions. Once his life and his complete work became a subject for open discussion and scrutiny his

---

[9] *Lorca's Late Poetry: A Critical Study* (Liverpool: Francis Cairns, 1990), 306.

mythic status changed: from Republican martyr to gay icon. Neither of these terms serves him well. Ignorance, willed or otherwise, yielded to overfamiliarity, to an open season for crude deconstructionists. At the same time, as if to compensate for his wretched fate at the hands of Nationalist thugs, there has emerged a rosy-tinted version of his life and character. Posterity may deem it necessary to adjust those judgements that presently overrate the man and underrate the work. Lorca was a victim not a martyr; a man of decent instincts, not a saint. He was generous and impulsive, but he could be vain and self-centred. One could excuse his lack of modesty for it would have been false. He towered over his contemporaries, and they knew it: he was fêted and lionized. Yet a later critical consensus, which looks to the achievements of the poetic group to which Lorca belonged, variously denominated the Poetic Group of 1925, the Generation of 1927, and the Generation of the Dictatorship, is apt to treat him at most as a first among equals. There is, however, surely no doubt that he is the most stylish and spectacular poet of twentieth-century Spain—a writer who fulfils most readily our expectations of what poetry can achieve.

NOTE ON THE TEXT AND TRANSLATION

THE Spanish texts are taken from the original volume collections, whose details of publication are provided in the Explanatory Notes at the back of the book.

The aim has been to provide a balanced selection of poems from all periods of Lorca's life. This has entailed including rather fewer poems than is usual in anthologies from the better-known books, notably *Romancero gitano* and *Poeta en Nueva York*, and instead finding more space for those from the earlier works. Such an emphasis, it is hoped, will both highlight Lorca's development as a poet and do justice to the somewhat underrated collections of the early to mid-1920s.

D. G. W.

Lorca's poetry poses the recognized problems of translation in an intense way. His Spanish is highly charged, culturally specific, strongly rhythmic, always musical. It evokes an ancient land, Andalusia, where Europe, Africa, and Arabia met and clashed. It evokes a world of searing heat, passions, and rough justice, resonating to the haunting sound of *cante jondo*, the purest form of Flamenco music. Here is a world which could scarcely be less Anglo-Saxon.

Lorca's work has been much translated in the decades since his death, so iconic a figure has he become. The translations in this volume have sought to render what might be called Lorca's *disposition*, and to give an account in English of the anguished, isolated sensibility that lies below the language of his poetry. My aim has been to produce angular, tight, uncluttered lines. Thanks to the stress system of Spanish, Lorca's sense of anguish and intensity is conveyed in a markedly accented metre; rhythmic pulse matches what is being voiced. Form and content become synonymous. However, too marked an English metrical foot might run the risk of lightness of tone quite at odds with Lorca's brittle urgency. Nor does Lorca use end-rhyme, another possible agreeable agent of security. Instead, he exploits the naturally occurring assonance of Spanish, which the English versions loosely have sought to reflect.

The first drafts of these translations were done at the Tyrone Guthrie Centre in Ireland during a residency funded by the EU in conjunction with the Irish Translators' and Interpreters' Association. My grateful thanks go to all three organizations. I would also like to thank my colleague, Gareth Walters, not only for his contribution to this venture, but for suggesting changes to the translation. I must thank the Heirs of Federico García Lorca for permission to publish this selection; and Bill Kosmas, acting on their behalf. Once more, Judith Luna has been a tactful and skilful editor. Chris and Fen Tyler saw to it that I received a scarce copy of the Green Horse Press's bilingual *Sonnets of Dark Love*—a generous gesture by them and Green Horse, much appreciated. Finally, to my wife Claire, who not only showed me much of Lorca's botany *in situ* during our Andalusian holidays, but also unobtrusively supported this project from first stirrings to bookshop shelf, go all my gratitude, all my love—and these translations.

M. S.

SELECT BIBLIOGRAPHY

Editions of Lorca's Work

Suites, ed. André Belamich (Barcelona: Ariel, 1983).

Libro de poemas, ed. Mario Hernández (Madrid: Alianza, 1984).

Poema del Cante Jondo; Romancero gitano, ed. Allen Josephs and Juan Caballero, 8th edn. (Madrid: Cátedra, 1985).

Canciones y primeras canciones, ed. Piero Menarini (Madrid: Espasa-Calpe, 1986).

Diván del Tamarit; Seis Poemas Galegos; Llanto por Ignacio Sánchez Mejías, ed. Andrew A. Anderson (Madrid: Espasa-Calpe, 1988).

Collected Poems, rev. bilingual edn., ed. Christopher Maurer (New York: Farrar, Strauss and Giroux, 2002).

Biography

Gibson, Ian, *The Death of Lorca* (London: Paladin, 1974).

—— *Federico García Lorca* (London and Boston: Faber and Faber, 1989).

Stainton, Leslie, *Lorca: A Dream of Life* (London: Bloomsbury, 1999).

Critical Studies

Anderson, Andrew A., *Lorca's Late Poetry: A Critical Study* (Leeds: Francis Cairns, 1990).

Bonaddio, Federico, 'Lorca's "Romance sonámbulo": The Desirability of Non-Disclosure', *Bulletin of Hispanic Studies*, 72 (1995), 385–401.

Dennis, Nigel, 'Lorca in the Looking-Glass: On Mirrors and Self-Contemplation', in C. Brian Morris (ed.), *'Cuando yo me muera': Essays in Memory of Federico García Lorca* (Lanham, Md., New York, and London: University Press of America, 1988), 41–55.

Gibson, Ian, 'Lorca's *Balada triste*: Children's Songs and the Theme of Sexual Disharmony in *Libro de poemas*', *Bulletin of Hispanic Studies*, 46 (1969), 21–38.

Harris, Derek, *García Lorca: Poeta en Nueva York*, Critical Guides to Spanish Texts, 24 (London: Grant & Cutler, 1978).

Loughran, David K., *Federico García Lorca: The Poetry of Limits* (London: Tamesis Books, 1978).

Morris, C. Brian (ed.), *Son of Andalusia: The Lyrical Landscapes of Federico García Lorca* (Nashville: Vanderbilt University Press, 1997).

Stanton, Edward F., *The Tragic Myth: Lorca and 'Cante Jondo'* (Lexington, Ky.: University of Kentucky Press, 1978).

Walters, D. Gareth, ' "Comprendí. Pero no explico": Revelation and Concealment in Lorca's *Canciones*', *Bulletin of Hispanic Studies*, 68 (1991), 265–79.

—— 'The Queen of Castile and the Andalusian Spinster: Lorca's Elegies for Two Women', in Robert Harvard (ed.), *Lorca: Poet and Playwright* (Cardiff and New York: University of Wales Press and St Martin's Press, 1992), 9–30.

—— *Canciones and the Early Poetry of Lorca: A Study in Critical Methodology and Poetic Maturity* (Cardiff: University of Wales Press, 2002).

Further Reading in Oxford World's Classics

Lorca, Federico García, *Four Major Plays*, trans. John Edmunds.

A CHRONOLOGY OF
FEDERICO GARCÍA LORCA

1898   Born in Fuentevaqueros in the vale of Granada.

1907   Family move to Asquerosa (setting for *Bernarda Alba*).

1909–19 Granada. Early musical studies, but enters University Faculty of Letters (1915). Among family friends are Socialist professor Fernando de los Ríos and composer Manuel de Falla.

1918   First book, *Impressions and Landscapes*, published.

1919–28 Based in Residencia de Estudiantes, Madrid. Friends there include Luis Buñuel, poets Jorge Guillén, Rafael Alberti (1924), and Salvador Dalí (1923).

1920   First play, *The Butterfly's Evil Spell*, performed.

1921   Publishes *Book of Poems*. Begins *Songs*, and the *cante jondo* poems.

1922   With Falla, organizes *cante jondo* festival in Granada.

1923   Begins *Mariana Pineda*, *Gypsy Ballads*, *The Prodigious Shoemaker's Wife*.

1924   José Moreno Villa shows him a description of *rosa mutabilis*.

1925–8 Close friendship and collaboration with Dalí. Growing interest in literary experiment: *Ode to Salvador Dalí*, *Buster Keaton's Walk*, *Love of Don Perlimplín and Belisa in her Garden*.

1927   Participates in Góngora tercentenary. Publishes *Songs*. *Mariana Pineda* performed (June). Exhibition of his drawings in Barcelona (July).

1928   *Gypsy Ballads* published. Rupture with Dalí. Reads press reports of Níjar murder case (kernal of *Blood Wedding*).

1929   Personal and artistic anxieties multiply. Goes to study at Columbia University (June). Experiences of New York, Wall Street crash, Black life of Harlem, evoke more radical forms of expression: Poet in *New York*, *The Public*.

1930   Travels to Cuba (March). *Yerma* in progress. In Madrid from June: reads the explicitly homosexual *The Public* to friends. *The Prodigious Shoemaker's Wife* performed (December).

1931   Writes *Once Five Years Pass*. Publishes *Poem of the Cante Jondo* Second Republic proclaimed in April.

1932–4   Director of travelling student theatre, 'La barraca' (part of Republican government's cultural outreach).

1932   Reads the complete *Blood Wedding* to friends (September).

1933   *Blood Wedding* performed (8 March). Theatre-club performance of *Don Perlimplín*. Centre-right government takes office in autumn. Lorca visits Argentina (September 1933–March 1934). Partial reading of *Yerma*. Meets cousin's former fiancé (story featured in *Doña Rosita*).

1934   Completes *Yerma* and *The Tamarit Divan*. Composes *Lament* for bullfighter Ignacio Sánchez Mejías, killed in August.

         Abortive October Revolution followed by repression. Lorca supports appeals for clemency. *Yerma* performed (29 December).

1935   *Lament for Ignacio Sánchez Mejías* published (May). Final drafting of *Poet in New York* (August). Signs anti-fascist manifesto (November). *Doña Rosita the Spinster* performed (12 December).

1936   Popular Front wins elections (16 February). Lorca signs appeal for peaceful co-operation. Joins in homage to Alberti (February), Luis Cernuda (April), and French Popular Front delegates (May). Writing *Sonnets of Dark Love*, and projects for theatre. *The House of Bernarda Alba* completed (19 June); read to friends (24 June).

         Political tension increases. Lorca travels to Granada on 13 July. Military uprising (17 July) seizes power in Granada (20–3 July). Mass arrests and killings.

         19 August: Lorca murdered by firing squad at Víznar.

SELECTED POEMS

Poemas de *Libro de Poemas*

Canción otoñal
Noviembre de 1918
(Granada)

Hoy siento en el corazón
un vago temblor de estrellas
pero mi senda se pierde
en el alma de la niebla.
La luz me troncha las alas
y el dolor de mi tristeza
va mojando los recuerdos
en la fuente de la idea.

Todas las rosas son blancas,
tan blancas como mi pena,
y no son las rosas blancas,
que ha nevado sobre ellas.
Antes tuvieron el iris.
También sobre el alma nieva.
La nieve del alma tiene
copos de besos y escenas
que se hundieron en la sombra
o en la luz del que las piensa.
La nieve cae de las rosas
pero la del alma queda,
y la garra de los años
hace un sudario con ella.

¿Se deshelará la nieve
cuando la muerte nos lleva?
¿O después habrá otra nieve
y otras rosas más perfectas?

¿Será la paz con nosotros
como Cristo nos enseña?

From *Book of Poems*

Autumn Song
November 1918
(Granada)

Today in my heart
a vague trembling of stars,
but my way is lost
in the soul of the mist.
Light lops my wings.
The hurt of my sadness
moistens memories
in thought's fountain.

All roses are white,
white as my pain,
white only when
snow's fallen on them.
Earlier they wore a rainbow.
Snow's also falling on the soul.
The soul's snow is kissed
by flakes and scenes
lost before in the shadow
or the light of the person thinking.
Snow falls from roses,
but remains on the soul,
and the year's thick needle
makes a shroud of them.

Will the snow melt
when death claims us?
Or will there be more snow
and more perfect roses?

Will we know peace
as Christ promises?

¿O nunca será posible
la solución del problema?

¿Y si el Amor nos engaña?
¿Quién la vida nos alienta
si el crepúsculo nos hunde
en la verdadera ciencia
del Bien que quizá no exista
y del Mal que late cerca?

Si la esperanza se apaga
y la Babel se comienza,
¿qué antorcha iluminará
los caminos en la Tierra?

Si el azul es un ensueño,
¿qué será de la inocencia?
¿Qué será del corazón
si el Amor no tiene flechas?

Y si la muerte es la muerte,
¿qué será de los poetas
y de las cosas dormidas
que ya nadie las recuerda?
¡Oh sol de las esperanzas!
¡Agua clara! ¡Luna nueva!
¡Corazones de los niños!
¡Almas rudas de las piedras!
Hoy siento en el corazón
un vago temblor de estrellas
y todas las rosas son
tan blancas como mi pena.

Or can it never be
for us?

And what if love's a trick?
Who'll salvage our lives
if gathering gloom buries us
in the certainty of Good,
unreal perhaps,
and of Evil throbbing very close?

What if hope dics
and Babel* rises?
What torch will light
earth's pathways?

If blue is dream
what then innocence?
What awaits the heart
if Love bears no arrows?

If death is death,
what then of poets
and the hibernating things
no one remembers?
Sun of our hopes!
Clear water! New moon!
Hearts of children!
Rough souls of the stones!
Today in my heart
a vague trembling of stars
and all roses are
as white as my pain.

Canción menor

Diciembre de 1918
(*Granada*)

Tienen gotas de rocío
las alas del ruiseñor,
gotas claras de la luna
cuajadas por su ilusión.

Tiene el mármol de la fuente
el beso del surtidor,
sueño de estrellas humildes.

Las niñas de los jardines
me dicen todas adiós
cuando paso. Las campanas
también me dicen adiós.
Y los árboles se besan
en el crepúsculo. Yo
voy llorando por la calle,
grotesco y sin solución,
con tristeza de Cyrano
y de Quijote,
        redentor
de imposibles infinitos
con el ritmo del reloj.
Y veo secarse los lirios
al contacto de mi voz
manchada de luz sangrienta,
y en mi lírica canción
llevo galas de payaso
empolvado. El amor
bello y lindo se ha escondido
bajo una araña. El sol
como otra araña me oculta
con sus patas de oro. No
conseguiré mi ventura,
pues soy como el mismo Amor,

Minor Song

December 1918
(*Granada*)

Dewdrops
on nightingale's wings,
clear droplets of moon
shaped by illusion.

On the fountain's marble
the waterspout's kiss,
dream of humble stars.

The girls in the gardens
all bid me farewell
as I pass. Bells too
bid me farewell
and trees kiss
in the half-light. I
go down the street weeping,
grotesque, no answers,
sad as Cyrano*
sad as Don Quixote,*
          redeeming
impossible infinites
with the rhythm of clocks.
I see irises dry
touched by my voice
bloodstained by light,
and in my lyric song
I wear the costume
of a grease-painted clown.
Beautiful marvellous love
hides under a spider. The sun
like another spider hides me
beneath its golden legs. I shan't
find happiness,
I'm like Love

cuyas flechas son de llanto,
y el carcaj el corazón.

Daré todo a los demás
y lloraré mi pasión
como niño abandonado
en cuento que se borró.

Balada triste

Pequeño poema

Abril de 1918
(*Granada*)

¡Mi corazón es una mariposa,
niños buenos del prado!,
que presa por la araña gris del tiempo
tiene el polen fatal del desengaño.

De niño yo canté como vosotros,
niños buenos del prado,
solté mi gavilán con las temibles
cuatro uñas de gato.
Pasé por el jardín de Cartagena,
la verbena invocando,
y perdí la sortija de mi dicha
al pasar el arroyo imaginario.

Fui también caballero
una tarde fresquita de Mayo.
Ella era entonces para mí el enigma,
estrella azul sobre mi pecho intacto.
Cabalgué lentamente hacia los cielos,
era un domingo de pipirigallo,
y vi que en vez de rosas y claveles
ella tronchaba lirios con sus manos.

Yo siempre fui intranquilo,
niños buenos del prado,

whose arrows are tears,
whose quiver the heart.

I'll give everything to others
and weep my passion
like the child abandoned
in a story crossed out.

Sad Ballad

Little poem

April 1918
(*Granada*)

My heart's a butterfly,
good children of the field,
pinned by time's grey spider,
filled with disillusionment's deadly pollen.

When I was a boy I sang like you,
good children of the field,
I let loose my sparrow-hawk
with its four frightful cat-claws.
I went through Cartagena's garden
imploring the verbena
and lost my good luck ring
when I crossed the invented stream.

I was a horseman too
one fresh afternoon in May.
She was my enigma then,
blue star on my unspoiled chest.
Slowly I rode towards the skies.
That Sunday of sainfoin
I saw her hands were cutting lilies
not roses and carnations.

Always I was restless,
good children of the field,

el *ella* del romance me sumía
en ensoñares claros.
¿Quién será la que coge los claveles
y las rosas de Mayo?
¿Y por qué la verán sólo los niños
a lomos de Pegaso?
¿Será esa misma la que en los rondones
con tristeza llamamos
Estrella, suplicándole que salga
a danzar por el campo?…

En abril de mi infancia yo cantaba,
niños buenos del prado,
la *ella* impenetrable del romance
donde sale Pegaso.
Yo decía en las noches la tristeza
de mi amor ignorado,
y la luna lunera, ¡qué sonrisa
ponía entre sus labios!
¿Quién será la que corta los claveles
y las rosas de Mayo?
Y de aquella chiquita, tan bonita,
que su madre ha casado,
¿en qué oculto rincón de cementerio
dormirá su fracaso?

Yo solo con mi amor desconocido,
sin corazón, sin llantos,
hacia el techo imposible de los cielos
con un gran sol por báculo.

¡Qué tristeza tan seria me da sombra!,
niños buenos del prado,
cómo recuerda dulce el corazón
los días ya lejanos…
¿Quién será la que corta los claveles
y las rosas de Mayo?

the *she* of the romance engulfed me
in limpid dreams:
who'll pick the May roses
and carnations?
Why will only the children
riding Pegasus* see her,
she who round here
with sadness we name
star, imploring her to come
and dance around the field?...

Good children of the field,
in the April of my childhood I sang
the impregnable *she* of the romance
where Pegasus rides out.
By night I told the sadness
of my unsuspected love —
and what a smile the moonish moon
wore on its lips!
Who'll cut the May roses
and carnations?
And that so pretty little girl,
given in marriage by her mother,
in what dark cemetery plot
will they lay her ruin?

I alone with my undiscovered love,
without heart, without tears,
towards the skies' impossible roof
with a huge sun to console me.

Such grave sadness shades me!
Good children of the field,
how sweet the heart's memories
of days so quickly done...
Who'll cut the May roses
and carnations?

Elegía

Diciembre de 1918
(*Granada*)

Como un incensario lleno de deseos,
pasas en la tarde luminosa y clara
con la carne oscura de nardo marchito
y el sexo potente sobre tu mirada.

Llevas en la boca tu melancolía
de pureza muerta, y en la dionisiaca
copa de tu vientre la araña que teje
el velo infecundo que cubre la entraña
nunca florecida con las vivas rosas,
fruto de los besos.

En tus manos blancas
llevas la madeja de tus ilusiones,
muertas para siempre, y sobre tu alma
la pasión hambrienta de besos de fuego
y tu amor de madre que sueña lejanas
visiones de cunas en ambientes quietos,
hilando en los labios lo azul de la nana.

Como Ceres dieras tus espigas de oro
si el amor dormido tu cuerpo tocara,
y como la virgen María pudieras
brotar de tus senos otra Vía Láctea.

Te marchitarás como la magnolia.
Nadie besará tus muslos de brasa.
Ni a tu cabellera llegarán los dedos
que la pulsen como las cuerdas de un arpa.

¡Oh mujer potente de ébano y de nardo!,
cuyo aliento tiene blancor de biznagas.
Venus del mantón de Manila que sabe
del vino de Málaga y de la guitarra.

Elegy

December 1918
(*Granada*)

Like a censer filled with desires,
you pass through clear evening,
flesh dark as spent spikenard;
your face pure sex.

On your mouth, dead chastity's
melancholy; in your womb's
Dionysian* chalice the spider weaves a barren veil
to hide flesh spurned by living roses,
the fruit of kisses.

In your white hands
the twist of lost illusions,
and on your soul a passion
hungry for kisses of fire,
and your mother-love dreaming distant
pictures of cradles in calm places,
lips spinning azure lullabies.

Like Ceres,* you'd offer golden corn
to have sleeping love touch your body;
to have another Milky Way
flow from your virgin breasts.

You'll wither like the magnolia.
No kisses burnt on your thighs,
no fingers in your hair,
playing it like a harp.

Woman strong with ebony and spikenard,
breath white as lilies,
Venus of the Manila shawl tasting
of Málaga wine and guitars!

¡Oh cisne moreno!, cuyo lago tiene
lotos de saetas, olas de naranjas
y espumas de rojos claveles que aroman
los nidos marchitos que hay bajo sus alas.

Nadie te fecunda. Mártir andaluza,
tus besos debieron ser bajo una parra
plenos del silencio que tiene la noche
y del ritmo turbio del agua estancada.

Pero tus ojeras se van agrandando
y tu pelo negro va siendo de plata;
tus senos resbalan escanciando aromas
y empieza a curvarse tu espléndida espalda.

¡Oh mujer esbelta, maternal y ardiente!
Virgen dolorosa que tiene clavadas
todas las estrellas del cielo profundo
en su corazón, ya sin esperanza.

Eres el espejo de una Andalucía
que sufre pasiones gigantes y calla,
pasiones mecidas por los abanicos
y por las mantillas sobre las gargantas
que tienen temblores de sangre, de nieve
y arañazos rojos hechos por miradas.

Te vas por la niebla del Otoño, virgen
como Inés, Cecilia y la dulce Clara,
siendo una bacante que hubiera danzado
de pámpanos verdes y vid coronada.

La tristeza inmensa que flota en tus ojos
nos dice tu vida rota y fracasada,
la monotonía de tu ambiente pobre
viendo pasar gente desde tu ventana,
oyendo la lluvia sobre la amargura
que tiene la vieja calle provinciana,
mientras que a lo lejos suenan los clamores
turbios y confusos de unas campanadas.

Black swan* on a lake of *saeta*
lotuses, waves of orange
and spray of red carnations scenting
the withered nests beneath its wings.

Andalusian martyr, left barren.
Your kisses should have been beneath a vine,
filled with night's silence,
stagnant water's cloudy rhythm.

But below your eyes circles start,
and your black hair turns silver.
Your breasts ease, spreading their scent
and your splendid shoulders start to stoop.

Slender woman, meant for motherhood, burning!
Virgin of sorrows;
forever hopeless heart
nailed by every star of the deep sky.

You're the mirror of an Andalusia
suffering and stifling great passions,
passions swaying to fans
and mantillas at throats
shivering with blood, with snow,
red scratch-marks of gazing eyes on them.

Like Inés,* Cecilia,* and sweet Clara,*
you go through autumn mists, a virgin,
a bacchante who'd have danced
in garlands of green shoots and vine.

The great sadness floating in your eyes
tells us your broken, shattered life,
the monotony of your bare world,
at your window watching people pass,
hearing rain fall on the bitterness
of the old provincial streets;
far away, a troubled clash of bells.

Mas en vano escuchaste los acentos del aire.
Nunca llegó a tu oído la dulce serenata.
Detrás de tus cristales aún miras anhelante.
¡Qué tristeza tan honda tendrás dentro del alma
al sentir en el pecho ya cansado y exhausto
la pasión de una niña recién enamorada!

Tu cuerpo irá a la tumba
intacto de emociones.
Sobre la oscura tierra
brotará una alborada.
De tus ojos saldrán dos claveles sangrientos
y de tus senos rosas como la nieve blancas.
Pero tu gran tristeza se irá con las estrellas
como otra estrella digna de herirlas y eclipsarlas.

Aire de nocturno

1919

Tengo mucho miedo
de las hojas muertas,
miedo de los prados
llenos de rocío.
Yo voy a dormirme;
si no me despiertas,
dejaré a tu lado mi corazón frío.

«¿Qué es eso que suena
muy lejos?»
«Amor,
el viento en las vidrieras,
¡amor mío!»

Te puse collares
con gemas de aurora.
¿Por qué me abandonas
en este camino?
Si te vas muy lejos

But you listened to the air's accents in vain.
The sweet serenade never reached you.
Behind your windows still you look and yearn.
The sadness that will flood your soul
when your wasted breast discovers
the passion of a girl new to love.

Your body will be buried
untouched by emotion.
A dawn song will spread
across the dark earth.
Two blood-red carnations will spring from your eyes,
and from your breasts, snow-white roses.
But your great sadness will join the stars,
a new star to wound and outshine the skies.

Nocturnal Air

1919

I'm petrified
by dead leaves,
by meadows
full of dew.
I'll sleep.
If you don't wake me,
I'll leave beside you my cold heart.

'What's that sound
so far away?'
'Love.
The wind on the panes,
my love!'

Round your neck I placed
the gems of dawn.
Why do you desert me
on this road?
If you go off so far

mi pájaro llora
y la verde viña
no dará su vino.

   «¿Qué es eso que suena
muy lejos?»
«Amor,
el viento en las vidrieras,
¡amor mío!»

   Tú no sabrás nunca,
esfinge de nieve,
lo mucho que yo
te hubiera querido
esas madrugadas
cuando tanto llueve
y en la rama seca
se deshace el nido.

   «¿Qué es eso que suena
muy lejos?»
«Amor,
el viento en las vidrieras,
¡amor mío!»

Canción primaveral
28 de marzo de 1919
(Granada)

I

   Salen los niños alegres
de la escuela,
poniendo en el aire tibio
del Abril, canciones tiernas.
¡Qué alegría tiene el hondo
silencio de la calleja!
Un silencio hecho pedazos
por risas de plata nueva.

my bird sobs,
and the green vineyard
won't give its wine.

'What's that sound
so far away?'
'Love.
The wind on the panes,
my love!'

You'll never know
how much I'd
have loved you,
snow-sphinx,
in those dawns
when it rains so hard
and the nest comes apart
on the dry branch.

'What's that sound
so far away?'
'Love.
The wind on the panes,
my love!'

Spring Song

28 March 1919
(*Granada*)

I

Happy children emerge
from school
sending tender songs
into mild April air.
Such joy for the deep
silence of the alleyway!
A silence smashed to pieces
by bright new silver laughter.

II

Voy camino de la tarde
entre flores de la huerta
dejando sobre el camino
el agua de mi tristeza.
En el monte solitario
un cementerio de aldea
parece un campo sembrado
con granos de calaveras.
Y han florecido cipreses
como gigantes cabezas
que con órbitas vacías
y verdosas cabelleras
pensativos y dolientes
el horizonte contemplan.

¡Abril divino, que vienes
cargado de sol y esencias,
llena con nidos de oro
las floridas calaveras!

Sueño

Mayo de 1919

Mi corazón reposa junto a la fuente fría.

(Llénalo con tus hilos,
araña del olvido.)

El agua de la fuente su canción le decía.

(Llénalo con tus hilos,
araña del olvido.)

Mi corazón despierto sus amores decía.

(Araña del silencio,
téjele tu misterio.)

II

I take the afternoon path
among orchard flowers
leaving on the way
the water of my sadness.
On the lonely hill
a village cemetery
looks like a field sown
with seeds of skulls.
Cypresses have flourished
like green-haired
hollow-socket
giant heads
pensive and in pain
contemplating the horizon.

Sacred April, now here
with your cargoes of essence and sun,
fill the flowering skulls
with nests of gold!

Dream

May 1919

My heart rests beside the cool fountain.

   (Fill it with your thread,
   spider of oblivion.)

The fountain water sang it its song.

   (Fill it with your thread,
   spider of oblivion.)

My wakened heart told of its loves.

   (Spider of silence
   spin it your mystery.)

El agua de la fuente lo escuchaba sombría.

(Araña del silencio,
téjele tu misterio.)

Mi corazón se vuelca sobre la fuente fría.

(¡Manos blancas, lejanas,
detened a las aguas!)

Y el agua se lo lleva cantando de alegría.

(¡Manos blancas, lejanas,
nada queda en las aguas!)

Balada de la placeta

1919

Cantan los niños
en la noche quieta:
¡Arroyo claro,
fuente serena!

LOS NIÑOS

¿Qué tiene tu divino
corazón en fiesta?

YO

Un doblar de campanas
perdidas en la niebla.

LOS NIÑOS

Ya nos dejas cantando
en la plazuela.
¡Arroyo claro,
fuente serena!

¿Qué tienes en tus manos
de primavera?

The shadowed water listened.

> (Spider of silence,
> spin it your mystery.)

My heart capsizes in the cold fountain.

> (White hands, far away,
> hold back the waters.)

And the water carries it off singing with joy.

> (White hands, far away,
> nothing remains in the waters!)

Ballad of the Little Square

1919

> In the still night
> the children sing.
> Clear stream,
> calm fountain!

THE CHILDREN

> What's in your festive
> godly heart?

I

> A toll of bells
> lost in mist.

THE CHILDREN

> Now you leave us singing
> on the little square,
> clear stream,
> calm fountain!

> What do you hold
> in your springtime hands?

YO

Una rosa de sangre
y una azucena.

LOS NIÑOS

Mójalas en el agua
de la canción añeja.
¡Arroyo claro,
fuente serena!

¿Qué sientes en tu boca
roja y sedienta?

YO

El sabor de los huesos
de mi gran calavera.

LOS NIÑOS

Bebe el agua tranquila
de la canción añeja.
¡Arroyo claro,
fuente serena!

¿Por qué te vas tan lejos
de la plazuela?

YO

¡Voy en busca de magos
y de princesas!

LOS NIÑOS

¿Quién te enseñó el camino
de los poetas?

YO

La fuente y el arroyo
de la canción añeja.

LOS NIÑOS

¿Te vas lejos, muy lejos
del mar y de la tierra?

I

A rose of blood
and a white lily.

THE CHILDREN

Wet them in the water
of the ancient song.
Clear stream,
calm fountain!

What's in your red
and thirsty mouth?

I

The bone-taste
of my great skull.

THE CHILDREN

Drink the calm water
of the ancient song.
Clear stream,
calm fountain!

Why do you stray so far
from the little square?

I

I go in search of sorcerers
and princesses!

THE CHILDREN

Who taught you the way
of the poets?

I

The stream and the fountain
of the ancient song.

THE CHILDREN

Are you going very, very far
from the sea and the earth?

YO

Se ha llenado de luces
mi corazón de seda,
de campanas perdidas,
de lirios y de abejas.
Y yo me iré muy lejos,
más allá de esas sierras,
más allá de los mares,
cerca de las estrellas,
para pedirle a Cristo
Señor que me devuelva
mi alma antigua de niño,
madura de leyendas,
con el gorro de plumas
y el sable de madera.

LOS NIÑOS

Ya nos dejas cantando
en la plazuela:
¡Arroyo claro,
fuente serena!

Las pupilas enormes
de las frondas resecas,
heridas por el viento,
lloran las hojas muertas.

La balada del agua del mar

1920

A Emilio Prados
(*cazador de nubes*)

El mar
sonríe a lo lejos.
Dientes de espuma,
labios de cielo.

—¿Qué vendes, oh joven turbia,
con los senos al aire?

I

My silk heart's
filled with lights,
lost bells,
lilies and bees,
and I'll go far,
further than these mountains,
further than the seas,
close to the stars
and I'll say to Christ,
Lord, give me back
the child's soul I once had,
steeped in legends,
with the feathered cap
and the wooden sabre.

THE CHILDREN

And now you leave us singing
on the little square,
clear stream,
calm fountain!

Huge pupils
of dried-out fronds,
wounded by the wind,
weep for dead leaves.

Seawater Ballad

1920

To Emilio Prados
(*hunter of clouds*)

The sea
smiles from afar.
Teeth of foam,
lips of sky.

'What do you sell, young,
troubled, bare-breasted woman?'

—Vendo, señor, el agua
de los mares.

—¿Qué llevas, oh negro joven,
mezclado con tu sangre?

—Llevo, señor, el agua
de los mares.

—¿Esas lágrimas salobres
de dónde vienen, madre?

—Lloro, señor, el agua
de los mares.

—Corazón, ¿y esta amargura
seria, de dónde nace?

—¡Amarga mucho el agua
de los mares!

El mar
sonríe a lo lejos.
Dientes de espuma,
labios de cielo.

Sueño

Mayo de 1919

Iba yo montado sobre
un macho cabrío.
El abuelo me habló
y me dijo:
«Ese es tu camino.»
«¡Es ése!», gritó mi sombra,
disfrazada de mendigo.
«¡Es aquel de oro!», dijeron
mis vestidos.
Un gran cisne me guiñó,

'Sir, the water of the seas.'

'What is it that's mixed, dark boy,
with your blood?'

'Sir, the water of the seas.'

'Where do those salt tears
come from, mother?'

'Sir, my eyes weep the water of the seas.'

'Heart, what is the source
of this grave bitterness?'

'The water of the seas
spreads a bitter cover!'

The sea
smiles from afar.
Teeth of foam,
lips of sky.

Dream

May 1919

I rode astride
a billy goat.
Grandfather said to me:
'Your way lies there.'
'Yes, yes', shouted my shadow,
dressed like a beggar.
My clothes said:
'It's paved with gold!'
A great swan winked and said:
'Follow me!'

diciendo: «¡Vente conmigo!»
Y una serpiente mordía
mi sayal de peregrino.

Mirando al cielo, pensaba:
«Yo no tengo camino.
Las rosas del fin serán
como las del principio.
En niebla se convierte
la carne y el rocío.»

Mi caballo fantástico me lleva
por un campo rojizo.
«¡Déjame!», clamó, llorando,
mi corazón pensativo.
Yo lo abandoné en la tierra,
lleno de tristeza.

Vino
la noche, llena de arrugas
y de sombras.

Alumbran el camino,
los ojos luminosos y azulados
de mi macho cabrío.

Otra canción

1919 (*Otoño*)

¡El sueño se deshizo para siempre!

En la tarde lluviosa
mi corazón aprende
la tragedia otoñal
que los árboles llueven.

Y en la dulce tristeza
del paisaje que muere

and a snake bit
my pilgrim smock.

   I looked at the sky and thought:
'Where is my path?
The last roses will be
like the first.
In the mist flesh
changes, and dew.'

   My fantasy horse bears me
over red land.
'Let me be!' my pensive heart
shouted, weeping.
I left it in the earth,
filled with sadness.

   Night came
full of folds
and shadows.

   The way is lit
by the luminous azure eyes
of my billy goat.

Another Song

1919 (Autumn)

   The dream came apart for good!

   In the rain-swept afternoon
my heart discovers
the tragedy of autumn
raining from the trees.

   And in the sweet sadness
of the dying landscape

mis voces se quebraron.
El sueño se deshizo para siempre.
¡Para siempre! ¡Dios mío!
Va cayendo la nieve
en el campo desierto
de mi vida,
y teme
la ilusión, que va lejos,
de helarse o de perderse.

¡Cómo me dice el agua
que el sueño se deshizo para siempre!
¿El sueño es infinito?
La niebla lo sostiene,
y la niebla es tan sólo
cansancio de la nieve.

Mi ritmo va contando
que el sueño se deshizo para siempre.
Y en la tarde brumosa
mi corazón aprende
la tragedia otoñal
que los árboles llueven.

El macho cabrío

1919

El rebaño de cabras ha pasado
junto al agua del río.
En la tarde de rosa y de zafiro,
llena de paz romantica,
yo miro
al gran macho cabrío.

¡Salve, demonio mudo!
Eres el más
intenso animal.

my voices cracked.
The dream came apart for good.
For good!
Snow's felling
on the barren field
of my life;
everywhere the dread
of freezing or getting lost.

   How the water tells me
that the dream came apart for good!
Dream without end?
The mist says so,
and the mist is just
the snow's respite.

   My rhythm's story is
that the dream came apart for good.
And in the misty afternoon
my heart discovers
the tragedy of autumn
raining from the trees.

The Billy Goat

1919

   The herd of goats passed where
the river flows.
In the sapphire pink afternoon
heavy with romantic peace,
I watch
the great billy goat.

   Greetings, mute demon,
you most intense of animals,
eternal mystic

Místico eterno
del infierno
carnal…

¡Cuántos encantos
tiene tu barba,
tu frente ancha,
rudo don Juan!
¡Qué gran acento el de tu mirada
mefistofélica
y pasional!

Vas por los campos
con tu manada
hecho un eunuco
¡siendo un sultán!
Tu sed de sexo
nunca se apaga;
¡bien aprendiste
del padre Pan!

La cabra,
lenta te va siguiendo,
enamorada con humildad;
mas tus pasiones son insaciables;
Grecia vieja
te comprenderá.

¡Oh ser de hondas leyendas santas,
de ascetas flacos y Satanás
con piedras negras y cruces toscas,
con fieras mansas y cuevas hondas
donde te vieron entre la sombra
soplar la llama
de lo sexual!

¡Machos cornudos
de bravas barbas!
¡Resumen negro a lo medieval!

of hell
made flesh...

   So many spells
in your beard,
on your broad brow,
you brute Don Juan!*
Such force
in those insane
Mephistophelian* eyes!

   You roam the fields
with your fellows,
emasculated
when you're really a sultan!
Your need of sex
is never satisfied.
Father Pan* taught you well!

   The nanny goat
follows you cautiously,
humble in her love;
but your passions have no boundaries;
Ancient Greece
would have understood.

   You come from the oldest Bible tales
of withered ascetics and Satan
with black stones, rude crosses,
tame beasts, and hollow caves
where in the shadows
they watched you
fan the flames of sex!

   Maleness
of wild beard and horn!
Dark emblems of the medieval world!

Nacisteis juntos con Filomnedes
entre la espuma casta del mar,
y vuestras bocas
la acariciaron
bajo el asombro del mundo astral.

Sois de los bosques llenos de rosas
donde la luz es huracán;
sois de los prados de Anacreonte,
llenos con sangre de lo inmortal.

¡Machos cabríos!
Sois metamórfosis
de viejos sátiros
perdidos ya.
Vais derramando lujuria virgen
como no tuvo otro animal.

¡Iluminados del Mediodía!
Pararse en firme
para escuchar
que desde el fondo de las campiñas
el gallo os dice:
«¡Salud!», al pasar.

You were born with Philommedes*
in the sea's chaste spray
which your mouths kissed
beneath astonished stars.

You come from rose-filled woods
of hurricane-light;
from Anacreon's* fields
swamped with immortal blood.

Billy goats,
metamorphosis
of old satyrs
gone for good!
Without another animal
you spill virgin lechery.

Luminous Southern beings!
Stand still to hear the cock
in a lost field
wish you God speed!
as you pass by.

Poemas de *Suites*

Canción con reflejo

En la pradera bailaba
mi corazón

(era la sombra
de un ciprés
sobre el viento)

y un árbol destrenzaba
la brisa del rocío.
¡La brisa!
Plata del tacto.

Yo decía: ¿recuerdas?

(No me importa
la estrella
ni la rosa.)

¿Recuerdas?

¡Oh palabra perdida!
¡Palabra
sin horizonte!

¿Recuerdas?...

En la pradera bailaba
mi corazón.

(Era la sombra
de un ciprés
en el viento.)

From *Suites*

Song with Reflection

In the meadow
my heart danced

(a cypress shadow
on the wind)

and a tree unplaited
the dew breeze.
Breeze,
silver to the touch!

I said: do you remember?

(The star
the rose
do not concern me.)

Remember?

Lost language!
Language
without horizons!

Remember?

In the meadow
my heart danced

(a cypress shadow
on the wind).

Sésamo

El reflejo
es lo real.
El río
y el cielo
son puertas que nos llevan
a lo Eterno.
Por el cauce de las ranas
o el cauce de los luceros
se irá nuestro amor cantando,
la mañana del gran vuelo.
Lo real
es el reflejo.
No hay más que un corazón
y un solo viento.
¡No llorar! Da lo mismo
estar cerca
que lejos.
Naturaleza es
el Narciso eterno.

Canción bajo lágrimas

En aquel sitio,
muchachita de la fuente,
que hay junto al río,
te quitaré la rosa
que te dio mi amigo,
y en aquel sitio,
muchachita de la fuente,
yo te daré mi lirio.
¿Por qué he llorado tanto?
¡Es todo tan sencillo!…
Esto lo haré ¿no sabes?
cuando vuelva a ser niño.
¡Ay! ¡ay!
Cuando vuelva a ser niño.

Sesame

The reflection is
what's real.
The river
and sky
are doors to take us
to the Eternal.
Down beds of frogs
or beds of bright stars
our love will go off, singing
the morning of the great flight.
The reflection is
what's real.
Only a heart remains,
only one wind.
Don't weep!
Near or far,
it's the same.
Eternal Narcissus,*
Nature's way.

Song beneath Tears

In that place,
little girl of the fountain,
that place by the river,
I'll take the rose
my friend gave you,
and in that place,
little girl of the fountain,
I'll give you my lily.
Why have I wept so much?
It's all so simple!
Surely you know that I'll do this
when I'm a child again,
Ay!
when I'm a child.

Paisaje sin canción

Cielo azul.
Campo amarillo.

Monte azul.
Campo amarillo.

Por la llanura tostada
va caminando un olivo.

Un solo
olivo.

Horizonte

Sobre la verde bruma
se cae un sol sin rayos.

La ribera sombría
sueña al par que la barca
y la esquila inevitable
traba la melancolía.

En mi alma de ayer
suena un tamborcillo
de plata.

Pescadores

El árbol gigantesco
pesca con sus lianas
topos raros
de la tierra.

El sauce sobre el remanso
se pesca sus ruiseñores.

Landscape without Song

Blue sky.
Yellow field.

Blue mountain.
Yellow field.

Across the scorched plain
an olive tree drifts.

One lone
olive
tree.

Horizon

A sun without rays
spills on green mist.

The shaded riverside
dreams at the pace of a boat
and the unavoidable bell
measures melancholy.

In my spent soul
the sound of a small
silver drum.

Fishermen

The giant tree's lianas
fish rare moles
from the earth.

Over the pool the willow
fishes nightingales

… pero en el anzuelo verde
del ciprés la blanca luna
no mordera… ni
tu corazón al mío,
morenita de Granada.

Delirio

Disuelta la tarde
y en silencio el campo,
los abejarucos
vuelan suspirando.
Los fondos deliran
azules y blancos.
El paisaje tiene
abiertos sus brazos.
¡Ay, señor, señor!
Esto es demasiado.

En el jardín de las toronjas de luna

Prólogo

Asy como la sombra nuestra vida se va,
que nunca más torna nyn de nos tornará

(Pero López de Ayala, *Consejos morales*)

Me he despedido de los amigos que más quiero para emprender un corto pero dramático viaje. Sobre un espejo de plata encuentro mucho antes de que amanezca el maletín con la ropa que debo usar en la extraña tierra a que me dirijo.

El perfume tenso y frío de la madrugada bate misteriosamente el inmenso acantilado de la noche.

En la página tersa del cielo temblaba la inicial de una nube, y debajo de mi balcón un ruiseñor y una rana levantan en el aire un aspa soñolienta de sonido.

Yo, tranquilo pero melancólico, hago los últimos preparativos, embargado por sutilísimas emociones de alas y círculos concéntricos.

… but the white moon won't take
the cypress's green bait…
nor your heart mine,
dark-haired girl of Granada.

Delirium

Fragmented evening,
field in silence.
Bee-eaters in flight,
a sigh.
Backcloth of blue and white
deliriums.
The landscape opens
its arms wide.
All too much,
Dear God!

In the Garden of Lunar Grapefruit

Prologue

And so like a shadow our life passes,
never to return, nor we.

(Pero López de Ayala, *Moral Counsels*)

I've said goodbye to the friends I love most in order to undertake a
short yet dramatic journey. Long before sunrise, I find on a silver
mirror the small case with the clothes I'll need in the strange coun-
try I'm making for.

The tense, cold scent of dawn mysteriously strikes the huge slop-
ing cliff of night.

On the stretched page of the sky, the trembling of a cloud's first
letter; beneath my balcony a nightingale and a frog raise high in the
air a drowsy cross of sound.

As for me, I'm quiet though full of melancholy; I make final prep-
arations, checked by the subtlest emotions of wings and concentric

Sobre la blanca pared del cuarto, yerta y rígida como una serpiente de museo, cuelga la espada gloriosa que llevó mi abuelo en la guerra contra el rey don Carlos de Borbón.

Piadosamente descuelgo esa espada, vestida de herrumbre amarillenta como un álamo blanco, y me la ciño recordando que tengo que sostener una gran lucha invisible antes de entrar en el jardín. Lucha extática y violentísima con mi enemigo secular, el gigantesco dragón del Sentido Común.

Una emoción aguda y elegíaca por las cosas que no han sido, buenas y malas, grandes y pequeñas, invade los paisajes de mis ojos casi ocultos por unas gafas de luz violeta. Una emoción amarga que me hace caminar hacia este jardín que se estremece en las altísimas llanuras del aire.

Los ojos de todas las criaturas golpean como puntos fosfóricos sobre la pared del porvenir… lo de atrás se queda lleno de maleza amarilla, huertos sin frutos y ríos sin agua. Jamás ningún hombre cayó de espaldas sobre la muerte. Pero yo, por un momento, contemplando ese paisaje abandonado e infinito, he visto planos de vida inédita, múltiples y superpuestos como los cangilones de una noria sin fin.

Antes de marchar siento un dolor agudo en el corazón. Mi familia duerme y toda la casa está en un reposo absoluto. El alba, revelando torres y contando una a una las hojas de los árboles, me pone un crujiente vestido de encaje lumínico.

Algo se me olvida… no me cabe la menor duda… ¡tanto tiempo preparándome! y… Señor, ¿qué se me olvida? ¡Ah! Un pedazo de madera… uno bueno de cerezo sonrosado y compacto.

Creo que hay que ir bien presentado… De una jarra con flores puesta sobre mi mesilla me prendo en el ojal siniestro una gran rosa pálida que tiene un rostro enfurecido pero hierático.

Ya es la hora.

(En las bandejas irregulares de las campanadas, vienen los kikirikis de los gallos.)

circles. On the white wall of my room, stiff and rigid like a snake in a museum, hangs the glory-covered sword my grandfather wielded in the war against Don Carlos the Pretender.*

Reverently, I take down the sword, coated in pale yellow rust like a white poplar, and I strap it on, remembering that I shall have to endure a great and invisible fight before I can enter the garden. A most violent, ecstatic fight against my secular enemy, the monster dragon called Common Sense.

A sharp elegy of nostalgia for things that have never been—good, bad, large, small—invades those landscapes of my eyes which my tinted glasses all but cancel. A bitter feeling that makes me head towards this garden shimmering on the highest plains of air.

The eyes of every creature throb like phosphorescent points against the wall of the future... the things of the past stay filled with yellow scrub, barren orchards, dried-up rivers. No man ever fell backwards into death. But I, briefly contemplating this abandoned, infinite landscape, see early sketches of the life unpublished, multiple and superimposed, like the scoops of an endless waterwheel.

Preparing to leave, I feel a needle of pain in my heart. My family is still asleep, and the whole house is in perfect repose. Dawn, revealing towers, and counting one by one the leaves of the trees, dresses me in glinting clothes of lace that crackle.

There's something I'm forgetting... I'm absolutely sure of it... so much time getting myself ready! And... Lord, what am I forgetting? Ah, yes, a scrap of wood... a nice piece of cherry wood, rose-coloured, tight-grained.

I believe in being well turned out when I travel... From a vase of flowers on my side-table, I select a large pale rose and pin it to my left lapel, a rose with an angry but hieratic face.

The time has come.

(In the clashing silverware of bells, the cockadoodledoos of the cockerels.)

Poemas de *Poema del Cante Jondo*

Paisaje

El campo
de olivos
se abre y se cierra
como un abanico.
Sobre el olivar
hay un cielo hundido
y una lluvia oscura
de luceros fríos.
Tiembla junco y penumbra
a la orilla del río.
Se riza el aire gris.
Los olivos
están cargados
de gritos.
Una bandada
de pájaros cautivos,
que mueven sus larguísimas
colas en lo sombrío.

La guitarra

Empieza el llanto
de la guitarra.
Se rompen las copas
de la madrugada.
Empieza el llanto
de la guitarra.
Es inútil
callarla.
Es imposible
callarla.
Llora monótona
como llora el agua,

From *Poem of the Cante Jondo*

Landscape

The field
of olive trees
opens and closes
like a fan.
Above the olive grove
a sunken sky,
and a cold dark rain
of morning-stars.
Half-light and rushes tremble
at the river's edge.
Grey air crinkles.
The olive trees
are freighted
with cries.
A flock
of captive birds
moves long long tails
in the gloom.

The Guitar

The guitar begins
to sob.
Dawn's drinking cups
smash.
The guitar begins
to sob.
You can't
make it stop.
Impossible
to silence it.
A monotone of sobs
like water,

como llora el viento
sobre la nevada.
Es imposible
callarla.
Llora por cosas
lejanas.
Arena del Sur caliente
que pide camelias blancas.
Llora flecha sin blanco,
la tarde sin mañana,
y el primer pájaro muerto
sobre la rama.
¡Oh guitarra!
Corazón malherido
por cinco espadas.

El grito

La elipse de un grito
va de monte
a monte.

Desde los olivos,
será un arco iris negro
sobre la noche azul.

¡Ay!

Como un arco de viola,
el grito ha hecho vibrar
largas cuerdas del viento.

¡Ay!

(Las gentes de las cuevas
asoman sus velones.)

¡Ay!

like wind
over snow.
Impossible
to silence it.
It sobs
for distant things.
Hot Southern sands
imploring white camellias.
It sobs for aimless arrow,
evening without morning,
and the first dead bird
on the branch.
O guitar!
Heart deep-wounded
by five swords.

The Shout

The shout,
an arc
from hill to hill.

A black rainbow will hang
from the olive trees
over blue night.

Ay!

Like a viola bow
the shout's made the wind's
long strings vibrate.

Ay!

(The cave-dwellers
bring out their lamps.)

Ay!

El silencio

Oye, hijo mío, el silencio.
Es un silencio ondulado,
un silencio,
donde resbalan valles y ecos
y que inclina las frentes
hacia el suelo.

El paso de la Siguiriya

Entre mariposas negras,
va una muchacha morena
junto a una blanca serpiente
de niebla.

Tierra de luz,
cielo de tierra.

Va encadenada al temblor
de un ritmo que nunca llega;
tiene el corazón de plata
y un puñal en la diestra.

¿Adónde vas, Siguiriya,
con un ritmo sin cabeza?
¿Qué luna recogerá
tu dolor de cal y adelfa?

Tierra de luz,
cielo de tierra.

Después de pasar

Los niños miran
un punto lejano.

Los candiles se apagan.
Unas muchachas ciegas

The Silence

My child, hear the silence.
An undulating silence,
a silence
of sliding valleys and echoes
tilting brows
towards the ground.

Dancing the *Siguiriya*

Among black butterflies
a dusky girl walks
with a white snake
of mist.

Earth of light,
sky of earth.

She's chained to the tremor
of a rhythm that never comes;
she has a heart of silver,
and in her right hand a dagger.

Where's that headless rhythm
leading you, *Siguiriya*?
What moon will gather in
your lime and oleander pain?

Earth of light,
sky of earth.

After Passing By

The children watch
a distant point.

Lamps go out.
Some blind girls

preguntan a la luna,
y por el aire ascienden
espirales de llanto.

Las montañas miran
un punto lejano.

Y después

Los laberintos
que crea el tiempo,
se desvanecen.

(Sólo queda
el desierto.)

El corazón,
fuente del deseo,
se desvanece.

(Sólo queda
el desierto.)

La ilusión de la aurora
y los besos,
se desvanecen.

Sólo queda
el desierto.
Un ondulado
desierto.

Tierra seca

Tierra seca,
tierra quieta
de noches
inmensas.

question the moon
and spirals of grief
rise in the air.

The mountains survey
a distant point.

And After

The labyrinths
formed by time
dissolve.

(Only desert
remains.)

The heart,
fountain of desire,
dissolves.

(Only desert
remains.)

The illusion of dawn
and kisses
dissolve.

Only desert
Remains.
Undulating
desert.

Parched Land

Parched land
quiet land
of huge
nights.

(Viento en el olivar,
viento en la sierra.)

Tierra
vieja
del candil
y la pena.
Tierra
de las hondas cisternas.
Tierra
de la muerte sin ojos
y las flechas.

(Viento por los caminos.
Brisa en las alamedas.)

Pueblo

Sobre el monte pelado,
un calvario.
Agua clara
y olivos centenarios.
Por las callejas
hombres embozados,
y en las torres
veletas girando.
Eternamente
girando.
¡Oh pueblo perdido
en la Andalucía del llanto!

Puñal

El puñal
entra en el corazón,
como la reja del arado
en el yermo.

(Wind in the olive grove,
wind on the sierra.)

Old
land
of lamps
and pain.
Land
of deep reservoirs.
Land
of death without eyes,
and arrows.

(Wind on the paths,
breeze among the poplars.)

Town

A Calvary
on the bare hilltop.
Clear water
and centenarian olive trees.
Down narrow streets
muffled men,
and on towers
spinning weathervanes.
Spinning
for ever.
O lost town
of Andalusia weeping!

Dagger

The dagger
enters the heart
like a plough
in dry soil.

No.
No me lo claves.
No.

El puñal,
como un rayo de sol,
incendia las terribles
hondonadas.

No.
No me lo claves.
No.

Encrucijada

Viento del Este,
un farol
y el puñal
en el corazón.
La calle
tiene un temblor
de cuerda
en tensión,
un temblor
de enorme moscardón.
Por todas partes
yo
veo el puñal
en el corazón.

¡Ay!

El grito deja en el viento
una sombra de ciprés.

(Dejadme en este campo
llorando.)

No.
Don't thrust it in me.
No.

The dagger
like a ray of sun
sets fire to awful
depths.

No.
Don't thrust it in me.
No.

Crossroads

East wind;
a lantern
and dagger
in the heart.
The street
vibrates
like stretched rope,
vibration
of a huge hornet.
Everywhere
I
see the dagger
in the heart.

Ay!

The shout leaves a cypress shadow
on the wind.

(Leave me in this field
weeping.)

Todo se ha roto en el mundo.
No queda más que el silencio.

(Dejadme en este campo
llorando.)

El horizonte sin luz
está mordido de hogueras.

(Ya os he dicho que me dejéis
en este campo
llorando.)

Sorpresa

Muerto se quedó en la calle
con un puñal en el pecho.
No lo conocía nadie.
¡Cómo temblaba el farol!
Madre.
¡Cómo temblaba el farolito
de la calle!
Era madrugada. Nadie
pudo asomarse a sus ojos
abiertos al duro aire.
Que muerto se quedó en la calle
que con un puñal en el pecho
y que no lo conocía nadie.

La Soleá

Vestida con mantos negros
piensa que el mundo es chiquito
y el corazón es inmenso.

Vestida con mantos negros.

Piensa que el suspiro tierno
y el grito, desaparecen
en la corriente del viento.

All in this world has broken.
All that's left is silence.

(Leave me in this field
weeping.)

The blackened horizon
is bitten by fires.

(I've told you to leave me
in this field
weeping.)

Surprise

He lay in the street, dead,
a dagger through his heart.
No one knew him.
How the lamp shook!
Mother.
How the little street–lamp shook!
It was dawn. No one
could meet his eyes,
open to the hard air.
For he lay in the street, dead,
a dagger through his heart,
and no one knew him.

The *Soleá*

Dressed in black cloaks
she thinks the world tiny,
the heart immense.

Dressed in black cloaks.

She thinks the soft whisper
and the shout vanish
carried off on the wind.

Vestida con mantos negros.

Se dejó el balcón abierto
y al alba por el balcón
desembocó todo el cielo.

¡Ay yayayayay,
que vestida con mantos negros!

Cueva

De la cueva salen
largos sollozos.

(Lo cárdeno
sobre lo rojo.)

El gitano evoca
países remotos.

(Torres altas y hombres
misteriosos.)

En la voz entrecortada
van sus ojos.

(Lo negro
sobre lo rojo.)

Y la cueva encalada
tiembla en el oro.

(Lo blanco
sobre lo rojo.)

Dressed in black cloaks.

The balcony was open
and at dawn the whole sky
spilt down through the balcony.

Ay ayayayay,
dressed in black cloaks!

Cave

From the cave
come long laments.

(Purple
on red.)

The gypsy conjures
distant lands.

(High towers and men
of mystery.)

His eyes move
to the cracked voice.

(Black
on red.)

And the whitewashed cave
trembles in gold.

(White
on red.)

Encuentro

Ni tú ni yo estamos
en disposición
de encontrarnos.
Tú… por lo que ya sabes.
¡Yo la he querido tanto!
Sigue esa verecita.
En las manos
tengo los agujeros
de los clavos.
¿No ves cómo me estoy
desangrando?
No mires nunca atrás,
vete despacio
y reza como yo
a San Cayetano,
que ni tú ni yo estamos
en disposición
de encontrarnos.

Alba

Campanas de Córdoba
en la madrugada.
Campanas de amanecer
en Granada.
Os sienten todas las muchachas
que lloran a la tierna
Soleá enlutada.
Las muchachas
de Andalucía la alta
y la baja.
Las niñas de España,
de pie menudo
y temblorosas faldas,
que han llenado de luces
las encrucijadas.

Meeting

You and I—
neither ready
to meet.
You… you know why.
I loved her so much!
Down this little path.
Nail-holes
in my hands.
Don't you see
my blood draining?
Never look behind you,
walk slowly away
and like me pray
To Saint Cayetano
for you and I,
neither's ready
to meet.

Dawn

Córdoba bells
at daybreak.
Dawn bells
in Granada.
All the girls weeping
to the tender, grieving *soleá*
recognize you.
The girls
of High Andalusia and Low.
Young girls of Spain
slight-footed shimmer-skirted
girls who've filled crossroads
with lights.
Córdoba bells
at daybreak,

¡Oh campanas de Córdoba
en la madrugada,
y oh campanas de amanecer
en Granada!

Arqueros

Los arqueros oscuros
a Sevilla se acercan.

Guadalquivir abierto.

Anchos sombreros grises,
largas capas lentas.

¡Ay, Guadalquivir!

Vienen de los remotos
países de la pena.

Guadalquivir abierto.

Y van a un laberinto.
Amor, cristal y piedra.

¡Ay, Guadalquivir!

Noche

Cirio, candil,
farol y luciérnaga.

La constelación
de la saeta.

Ventanitas de oro
tiemblan,
y en la aurora se mecen
cruces superpuestas.

and dawn bells
in Granada!

Bowmen

The dark bowmen
close in on Seville.

*Spreading Guadalquivir.**

Grey broad-brimmed hats,
long slow capes.

Ay, Guadalquivir!

They come from far
countries of pain.

Spreading Guadalquivir.

And head for a labyrinth.
Love, glass, stone.

Ay, Guadalquivir!

Night

Lamp, candle,
firefly, lantern.

The *saeta*'s
constellation.

Little windows of gold
tremble,
and in the dawn the sway
of cross upon cross.

Cirio, candil,
farol y luciérnaga.

Sevilla

Sevilla es una torre
llena de arqueros finos.

Sevilla para herir.
Córdoba para morir.

Una ciudad que acecha
largos ritmos.
y los enrosca
como laberintos.
Como tallos de parra
encendidos.

¡Sevilla para herir!

Bajo el arco del cielo,
sobre su llano limpio,
dispara la constante
saeta de su río.

¡Córdoba para morir!

Y loca de horizonte,
mezcla en su vino
lo amargo de Don Juan
y lo perfecto de Dionisio.

Sevilla para herir.
¡Siempre Sevilla para herir!

Lamp, candle,
firefly, lantern.

Seville

Seville is a tower
full of fine bowmen.

Seville for wounds
Córdoba for death.

A city that snares
slow rhythms
and twists them
like labyrinths
like vine-shoots,
blazing.

Seville for wounds!

Beneath the sky's arc,
over its clean plain,
the constant *saeta*
dart of the river.

Córdoba for death!

Mad with horizon,
it mixes in its wine
Don Juan's bitterness
and the perfection of Dionysus.

Seville for wounds!
Always Seville for wounds!

Procesión

Por la calleja vienen
extraños unicornios.
¿De qué campo,
de qué bosque mitológico?
Más cerca,
ya parecen astrónomos.
Fantásticos Merlines
y el Ecce Homo,
Durandarte encantado,
Orlando furioso.

Paso

Virgen con miriñaque,
Virgen de la Soledad,
abierta como un inmenso
tulipán.
En tu barco de luces
vas
por la alta marea
de la ciudad,
entre saetas turbias
y estrellas de cristal.
Virgen con miriñaque,
tú vas
por el río de la calle,
¡hasta el mar!

Saeta

Cristo moreno
pasa
de lirio de Judea
a clavel de España.

Procession

Down alleyways
come strange unicorns.
From what field
what mythic wood?
Closer to
they seem like astronomers.
Fantastic Merlins,*
the Ecce Homo,*
enchanted Durandarte,*
Orlando furioso.*

Float, Holy Week

Virgin with crinoline,
Virgin of Solitude,
open like a gigantic
tulip.
In your boat of lights
you move
on the high tide
of the city
among smoky *saetas*
and stars of glass.
Virgin with crinoline,
you move
down the river of the street
and out to the sea!

Saeta

Dark Christ
passes
from lily of Judaea
to carnation of Spain.

¡Miradlo por dónde viene!

De España.
Cielo limpio y oscuro,
tierra tostada,
y cauces donde corre
muy lenta el agua.
Cristo moreno,
con las guedejas quemadas,
los pómulos salientes
y las pupilas blancas.

¡Miradlo por dónde va!

Balcón

La Lola
canta saetas.
Los toreritos
la rodean,
y el barberillo,
desde su puerta,
sigue los ritmos
con la cabeza.
Entre la albahaca
y la hierbabuena,
la Lola canta
saetas.
La Lola aquella,
que se miraba
tanto en la alberca.

Madrugada

Pero como el amor
los saeteros
están ciegos.

*See where he comes!**

Of Spain.
Clean dark sky,
Sun-browned earth,
and riverbeds whose water
creeps by.
Dark Christ,
scorched locks of hair
high cheekbones
and white pupils.

See where he goes!

Balcony

Lola
sings *saetas*.
Pretend *toreros*
circle round,
and from his doorway
the little barber
nods his head
in rhythm.
Among the basil
and mint,
Lola sings
saetas.
Lola, she
who gazed at herself
for so long in the pool.

Dawn

But like love's
arrows, *saetas*
fly blind.

Sobre la noche verde,
las saetas
dejan rastros de lirio
caliente.

La quilla de la luna
rompe nubes moradas
y las aljabas
se llenan de rocío.

¡Ay, pero como el amor
los saeteros
están ciegos!

Saetas,
burning lily
streaking green night.

The keel of the moon
breaks mulberry clouds
and quivers
fill with dew.

Ay, but like love's
arrows, *saetas*
fly blind!

Poemas de *Canciones*

Nocturnos de la ventana

A la memoria de José de Ciria y Escalante. Poeta

1

Alta va la luna.
Bajo corre el viento.

(Mis largas miradas,
exploran el cielo.)

Luna sobre el agua.
Luna bajo el viento.

(Mis cortas miradas
exploran el suelo.)

Las voces de dos niñas
venían. Sin esfuerzo,
de la luna del agua,
me fui a la del cielo.

2

Un brazo de la noche
entra por mi ventana.

Un gran brazo moreno
con pulseras de agua.

Sobre un cristal azul
jugaba al río mi alma.

Los instantes heridos
por el reloj… pasaban.

From *Songs*

Nocturnes at the Window

To the memory of José de Ciria y Escalante. Poet

I

The moon rides high.
The wind runs below.

(My sweeping gaze
explores the sky.)

Moon on water.
Moon below the wind.

(My close gaze
explores the ground.)

Two girls' voices
approached. Easily
I went from the water's moon
to the moon in the sky.

2

An arm of night
comes through my window.

A great dark arm
wearing bracelets of water.

On blue crystal
my soul played at rivers.

Moments wounded
by the clock... passed by.

3

Asomo la cabeza
por mi ventana, y veo
cómo quiere cortarla
la cuchilla del viento.

En esta guillotina
invisible, yo he puesto
las cabezas sin ojos
de todos mis deseos.

Y un olor de limón
llenó el instante inmenso,
mientras se convertía
en flor de gasa el viento.

4

Al estanque se le ha muerto
hoy una niña de agua.
Está fuera del estanque,
sobre el suelo amortajada.

De la cabeza a sus muslos
un pez la cruza, llamándola.
El viento le dice «Niña»,
mas no puede despertarla.

El estanque tiene suelta
su cabellera de algas
y al aire sus grises tetas
estremecidas de ranas.

«Dios te salve» rezaremos
a Nuestra Señora de Agua
por la niña del estanque
muerta bajo las manzanas.

Yo luego pondré a su lado
dos pequeñas calabazas
para que se tenga a flote,
¡ay! sobre la mar salada.

3

I put my head
out of my window and see
how much the wind's knife
wants to slice it off.

On this unseen
guillotine, I've placed
the eyeless head
of all my desires.

And the lemon scent
filled the immense moment
while the wind became
a bloom of gauze.

4

There today in the pond
a water girl has found death.
Pulled from the pond,
she's laid out in a shroud.

From her head to her thighs
a fish crosses, calling her name.
The wind says 'child',
but can't wake her.

The pond has shaken out
her seaweed hair,
her grey bared teats
trembling with frogs.

God keep you. We'll pray
to Our Lady of Water
for the girl in the pond
under the apples, dead.

Later I'll place two small gourds
beside her so she may float
on the salt sea.
    Ay!

Canción tonta

Mamá.
Yo quiero ser de plata.

Hijo,
tendrás mucho frío.

Mamá.
Yo quiero ser de agua.

Hijo,
tendrás mucho frío.

Mamá.
Bórdame en tu almohada.

¡Eso sí!
¡Ahora mismo!

Canción de jinete

Córdoba.
Lejana y sola.

Jaca negra, luna grande,
y aceitunas en mi alforja.
Aunque sepa los caminos
yo nunca llegaré a Córdoba.

Por el llano, por el viento,
jaca negra, luna roja.
La muerte me está mirando
desde las torres de Córdoba.

¡Ay, qué camino tan largo!
¡Ay, mi jaca valerosa!

Foolish Song

Mama,
I want to turn into silver.

Son,
you'd freeze.

Mama,
I want to turn into water.

Son,
you'd freeze.

Mama,
sew me into your pillow.

This time yes,
and straightaway!

Horseman's Song

Córdoba,
alone and far.

Black pony, large moon,
olives in my saddlebag.
Though I know the way
I'll never get to Córdoba.

Through the wind, across the plain,
black pony, red moon.
Death is watching me
from the towers of Córdoba.

Such a long road!
My valiant mount!

¡Ay, que la muerte me espera,
antes de llegar a Córdoba!

Córdoba.
Lejana y sola.

¡Es verdad!

¡Ay, qué trabajo me cuesta
quererte como te quiero!

Por tu amor me duele el aire,
el corazón
y el sombrero.

¿Quién me compraría a mí,
este cintillo que tengo
y esta tristeza de hilo
blanco, para hacer pañuelos?

¡Ay qué trabajo me cuesta
quererte como te quiero!

Verlaine

La canción,
que nunca diré,
se ha dormido en mis labios.
La canción,
que nunca diré.

Sobre las madreselvas
había una luciérnaga,
y la luna picaba
con un rayo en el agua.

Entonces yo soñé,
la canción,
que nunca diré.

Death awaits me
before I get to Córdoba!

Córdoba,
alone and far.

It's true!

What it costs me
to love you as I do!

Air hurts me,
heart,
hat,
loving you.

Who'll buy my hatband,
this sadness of white thread,
and turn them into handkerchiefs?

What it costs me
to love you as I do!

Verlaine

The song
I'll never sing
fell silent on my lips.
The song
I'll never sing.

A firefly
was on the honeysuckle
and a moonbeam
stabbed the water.

So then I dreamt
the song
I'll never sing.

Canción llena de labios
y de cauces lejanos.

Canción llena de horas
perdidas en la sombra.

Canción de estrella viva
sobre un perpetuo día.

Baco

Verde rumor intacto.
La higuera me tiende sus brazos.

Como una pantera, su sombra,
acecha mi lírica sombra.

La luna cuenta los perros.
Se equivoca y empieza de nuevo.

Ayer, mañana, negro y verde,
rondas mi cerco de laureles.

¿Quién te querría como yo,
si me cambiaras el corazón?

… Y la higuera me grita y avanza
terrible y multiplicada.

Juan Ramón Jiménez

En el blanco infinito,
nieve, nardo y salina,
perdió su fantasía.

El color blanco, anda,
sobre una muda alfombra
de plumas de paloma.

Song filled with lips,
welling up from afar.

Song filled with hours
counted off in the shade.

Song of the star alive
above perpetual day.

Bacchus

Green murmur, intact.
The fig tree spreads out its arms to me.

Like a panther, it shadows
my lyrical shadow.

The moon counts dogs,
gets lost and starts again.

Yesterday, tomorrow, black and green,
you circle my laurel wreath.

If only you changed my heart,
I'd love you like nobody else.

... The fig tree shouts at me, advancing,
fearsome multiplicity.

Juan Ramón Jiménez

In the infinite white,
snow, salt-flat, spikenard,
his imagination went.

On then, colour white,
across a soundless carpet
of pigeon feathers.

Sin ojos ni ademán
inmóvil sufre un sueño.
Pero tiembla por dentro.

En el blanco infinito,
¡qué pura y larga herida
dejó su fantasía!

En el blanco infinito.
Nieve. Nardo. Salina.

Venus

Así te vi

La joven muerta
en la concha de la cama,
desnuda de flor y brisa
surgía en la luz perenne.

Quedaba el mundo,
lirio de algodón y sombra,
asomado a los cristales
viendo el tránsito infinito.

La joven muerta,
surcaba el amor por dentro.
Entre la espuma de las sábanas
se perdía su cabellera.

Debussy

Mi sombra va silenciosa
por el agua de la acequia.

Por mi sombra están las ranas
privadas de las estrellas.

La sombra manda a mi cuerpo
reflejos de cosas quietas.

No eyes, no gesture, motionless,
a dream plagues him.
But inside he trembles.

In the infinite white,
the pure white wound
his imagination left!

In the infinite white.
Snow. Salt-flat. Spikenard.

Venus

I saw you thus

The young woman, dead,
in the shell of the bed,
stripped of breeze and flowers
rose into undimmed light.

The world remained,
a lily of cotton and shade,
through window panes
watching the infinite transit.

The young woman, dead,
proffered love from within.
Her hair vanished
in the foam of sheets.

Debussy

My shadow moves silently
down the coursing water.

My shadow deprives the frogs
of stars.

The shadow sends my body
reflections of still things.

Mi sombra va como inmenso
cínife color violeta.

Cien grillos quieren dorar
la luz de la cañavera.

Una luz nace en mi pecho,
reflejado, de la acequia.

Narciso

Niño.
¡Que te vas a caer al río!

En lo hondo hay una rosa
y en la rosa hay otro río.

¡Mira aquel pájaro! ¡Mira
aquel pájaro amarillo!

Se me han caído los ojos
dentro del agua.

¡Dios mío!
¡Que se resbala! ¡Muchacho!

… y en la rosa estoy yo mismo.

Cuando se perdió en el agua,
comprendí. Pero no explico.

Al oído de una muchacha

No quise.
No quise decirte nada.

Vi en tus ojos
dos arbolitos locos.
De brisa, de risa y de oro.

My shadow moves like a huge
violet gnat.

A hundred crickets try to gild
the light of the reeds.

A new glow in my breast,
reflected from the water.

Narcissus

Child!
You'll fall in the river!

In the depths there's a rose
and in the rose another river.

See that bird! Look
at that yellow bird!

My eyes have disappeared
into the water.

Oh!
He's slipping! Little boy!

… and I myself am in the rose.

When he was lost in the water
I understood. But I shan't explain.

In a Girl's Ear

I didn't want to.
I didn't want to tell you a thing.

In your eyes I saw
two mad little trees.
Of air, of laughter, of gold.

Se meneaban.

No quise.
No quise decirte nada.

La luna asoma

Cuando sale la luna
se pierden las campanas
y aparecen las sendas
impenetrables.

Cuando sale la luna,
el mar cubre la tierra
y el corazón se siente
isla en el infinito.

Nadie come naranjas
bajo la luna llena.
Es preciso comer,
fruta verde y helada.

Cuando sale la luna
de cien rostros iguales,
la moneda de plata
solloza en el bolsillo.

Murió al amanecer

Noche de cuatro lunas
y un solo árbol,
con una sola sombra
y un solo pájaro.

Busco en mi carne las
huellas de tus labios.
El manantial besa al viento
sin tocarlo.

They swayed.

I didn't want to.
I didn't want to tell you a thing.

The Moon Appears

When the moon rises
bells are lost
and impenetrable
paths appear.

When the moon rises,
sea covers land
and the heart feels like
an island in infinity.

No one eats oranges
beneath a full moon.
Ice-cold green fruit
is right.

When the moon rises,
with the same hundred faces,
silver coins
sob in purses.

He Died at Dawn

Night of four moons
and a single tree
with a single shadow
and a single bird.

I search my flesh for the
mark of your lips.
The fountain kisses the wind
without touching it.

Llevo el No que me diste,
en la palma de la mano,
como un limón de cera
casi blanco.

Noche de cuatro lunas
y un solo árbol.
En la punta de una aguja,
está mi amor ¡girando!

Primer aniversario

La niña va por mi frente.
¡Oh, qué antiguo sentimiento!

¿De qué me sirve, pregunto,
la tinta, el papel y el verso?

Carne tuya me parece,
rojo lirio, junco fresco.

Morena de luna llena.
¿Qué quieres de mi deseo?

Segundo aniversario

La luna clava en el mar
un largo cuerno de luz.

Unicornio gris y verde,
estremecido pero extático.

El cielo flota sobre el aire
como una inmensa flor de loto.

(¡Oh, tú sola paseando
la última estancia de la noche!)

The *No* you told me I bear
in the palm of my hand
like an off-white
wax lemon.

Night of four moons
and a single tree.
On the point of a needle
there's my love
spinning!

First Anniversary

The girl passes across my brow.
Ancient, ancient feeling!

What use to me, I ask,
are paper, verse, ink?

To me your flesh is
red lily, cool reed.

Dark girl of the full moon.
What do you want of my desire?

Second Anniversary

The moon nails to the sea
a large horn of light.

Green and grey unicorn,
shuddering yet ecstatic.

Sky floating on the air
like an enormous lotus flower.

(You alone patrolling
the last station of night!)

Lucía Martínez

Lucía Martínez.
Umbría de seda roja.

Tus muslos como la tarde
van de la luz a la sombra.
Los azabaches recónditos
oscurecen tus magnolias.

Aquí estoy, Lucía Martínez.
Vengo a consumir tu boca
y arrastrarte del cabello
en madrugada de conchas.

Porque quiero, y porque puedo.
Umbría de seda roja.

La soltera en misa

Bajo el moisés del incienso,
adormecida.

Ojos de toro te miraban.
Tu rosario llovía.

Con ese traje de profunda seda,
no te muevas, Virginia.

Da los negros melones de tus pechos
al rumor de la misa.

Malestar y noche

Abejaruco.
En tus árboles oscuros.
Noche de cielo balbuciente
y aire tartamudo.

Lucía Martínez

Lucía Martínez.
Shadow of red silk.

Your thighs like evening
move from light to shade.
Hidden jet darkens
your magnolias.

I am here, Lucía Martínez,
here to consume your mouth
and drag you by the hair
into the seashell dawn.

Because I want to, because I can.
Red silk shadow.

The Spinster at Mass

Beneath the cradle of incense,
asleep.

Eyes of bulls watched you.
Your rosary rained.

In that dress of deep silk,
Virginia, do not move.

Offer your dark melon breasts
to the murmur of the Mass.

Malaise and Night

Bee-eater
in your dark trees.
Night of babbling sky
and stuttering air.

Tres borrachos eternizan
sus gestos de vino y luto.
Los astros de plomo giran
sobre un pie.
    Abejaruco.
En tus árboles oscuros.

Dolor de sien oprimida
con guirnalda de minutos.
¿Y tu silencio? Los tres
borrachos cantan desnudos.

Pespunte de seda virgen
tu canción.
    Abejaruco.
Uco uco uco uco.
    Abejaruco.

Desposorio

Tirad ese anillo
al agua.

(La sombra apoya sus dedos
sobre mi espalda.)

Tirad ese anillo. Tengo
más de cien años. ¡Silencio!

¡No preguntadme nada!

Tirad ese anillo
al agua.

Three drunks perpetuate
their movements of wine and sorrow.
Leaden astral bodies spin
on one foot.
    Bee-eater
in your dark trees.

Aching temple clamped
by a garland of minutes.
And your silence? The three nude
drunks sing.

Back-stitch of pure silk,
your song.
    Bee-eater
Ooco, ooco, ooco, ooco.
    Bee-eater.

Betrothal

Throw this ring
to the water.

(The shade places fingers
on my back.)

Throw this ring. I am
more than a hundred years old. Quiet!

Ask me nothing!

Throw this ring
to the water.

Despedida

Si muero,
dejad el balcón abierto.

El niño come naranjas.
(Desde mi balcón lo veo.)

El segador siega el trigo.
(Desde mi balcón lo siento.)

¡Si muero,
dejad el balcón abierto!

En el instituto y en la universidad

La primera vez
no te conocí.
La segunda, sí.

Dime
si el aire te lo dice.

Mañanita fría
yo me puse triste,
y luego me entraron
ganas de reírme.

No te conocí.
Sí me conociste.
Sí te conocí.
No me conociste.

Ahora entre los dos
se alarga impasible,
un mes, como un
biombo de días grises.

Parting

If I die
leave the balcony open.

The boy eats oranges.
(From my balcony I see him.)

The reaper cuts the wheat.
(From my balcony I hear him.)

If I die,
leave the balcony open!

In the Institute and in the University

The first time
I didn't know you.
The second time I did.

Tell me
if the air tells you so.

One sharp morning
I grew sad
and was seized
by the impulse to laugh.

I didn't know you.
But you knew me.
Yes I knew you.
You didn't know me.

Now a month stretches
between us two,
no feeling,
like a screen of grey days.

La primera vez
no te conocí.
La segunda, sí.

Madrigalillo

Cuatro granados
tiene tu huerto.

(Toma mi corazón
nuevo.)

Cuatro cipreses
tendrá tu huerto.

(Toma mi corazón
viejo.)

Sol y luna.
Luego…
¡ni corazón,
ni huerto!

Preludio

Las alamedas se van,
pero dejan su reflejo.

Las alamedas se van,
pero nos dejan el viento.

El viento está amortajado
a lo largo bajo el cielo.

Pero ha dejado flotando
sobre los ríos, sus ecos.

El mundo de las luciérnagas
ha invadido mis recuerdos.

The first time
I didn't know you.
The second time I did.

Light Madrigal

Four pomegranate trees
in your orchard.

(Take my new
heart.)

There'll be four cypress trees
in your orchard.

(Take my old
heart.)

Sun and moon.
Then, afterwards...
Neither heart
nor orchard!

Prelude

The avenues of poplar go
but leave their reflection.

The avenues of poplar go
but leave us the wind.

The shrouded wind lies
full length beneath the sky.

But it's left its echoes
floating on rivers.

The world of fireflies
has invaded my memories.

Y un corazón diminuto
me va brotando en los dedos.

De otro modo

La hoguera pone al campo de la tarde,
unas astas de ciervo enfurecido.
Todo el valle se tiende; por sus lomos,
caracolea el vientecillo.

El aire cristaliza bajo el humo.
Ojo de gato triste y amarillo.
Yo en mis ojos paseo por las ramas.
Las ramas se pasean por el río.

Llegan mis cosas esenciales.
Son estribillos de estribillos.
Entre los juncos y la baja-tarde,
¡qué raro que me llame Federico!

Canción de noviembre y abril

El cielo nublado
pone mis ojos blancos.

Yo, para darles vida,
les acerco una flor
amarilla.

No consigo turbarlos.
Siguen yertos y blancos.

(Entre mis hombros vuela
mi alma dorada y plena.)

El cielo de abril
pone mis ojos de añil.

And a tiny, tiny heart
is growing from my fingers.

Another Way

On the evening land the bonfire lays
the antlers of a maddened stag.
The valley spreads out. A gambolling breeze
skips among its folds.

Air crystallizes under the smoke.
— sad yellow cat's eye—
Inside my eyes I drift among the branches.
The branches drift down river.

Things vital to me appear.
Refrains of refrains.
Among the reeds and the falling day,
how strange my name should be Federico!

Song of November and April

The cloudy sky
blanks out my eyes.

To restore them, I
place a yellow flower
next to them.

I can't change them.
They remain lifeless, blank.

(Between my shoulders
my full and golden soul takes wing.)

The April sky
turns my eyes indigo.

Yo, para darles alma,
les acerco una rosa
blanca.

No consigo infundir
lo blanco en el añil.

(Entre mis hombros vuela
mi alma impasible y ciega.)

Canción del naranjo seco

A Carmen Morales

Leñador.
Córtame la sombra.
Líbrame del suplicio
de verme sin toronjas.

¿Por qué nací entre espejos?
El día me da vueltas.
Y la noche me copia
en todas sus estrellas.

Quiero vivir sin verme.
Y hormigas y vilanos,
soñaré que son
mis hojas y mis pájaros.

Leñador.
Córtame la sombra.
Líbrame del suplicio
de verme sin toronjas.

To give them a soul, I
place a white rose
next to them.

I can't make white
blend with indigo.

(Between my shoulders
my blind and stony soul takes wing.)

Song of the Dry Orange Tree

To Carmen Morales

Woodsman,
chop down my shadow.
Free me from the torture
of not bearing fruit.

Why was I born among mirrors?
Around me day dances
and night copies me
onto her stars.

I want to live blind to myself.
And I'll dream
that ants and burrs
are my leaves and my birds.

Woodsman,
chop down my shadow.
Free me from the torture
of not bearing fruit.

Poemas de *Romancero gitano*

Romance de la luna, luna

A Conchita García Lorca

La luna vino a la fragua
con su polisón de nardos.
El niño la mira, mira.
El niño la está mirando.
En el aire conmovido
mueve la luna sus brazos
y enseña, lúbrica y pura,
sus senos de duro estaño.
—Huye luna, luna, luna.
Si vinieran los gitanos,
harían con tu corazón
collares y anillos blancos.
—Niño, déjame que baile.
Cuando vengan los gitanos,
te encontrarán sobre el yunque
con los ojillos cerrados.
—Huye luna, luna, luna,
que ya siento sus caballos.
—Niño, déjame, no pises
mi blancor almidonado.

El jinete se acercaba
tocando el tambor del llano.
Dentro de la fragua el niño
tiene los ojos cerrados.
Por el olivar venían,
bronce y sueño, los gitanos.
Las cabezas levantadas
y los ojos entornados.

Cómo canta la zumaya,
¡ay, cómo canta en el árbol!

From *Gypsy Ballads*

Ballad of the Moon, the Moon

To Conchita García Lorca

The moon came to the forge
wearing her bustle of bulbs.
The boy's looking at her,
looking and looking.
In the disturbed air
the moon moves her arms,
and lewd and pure, lifts
her hard metallic breasts.
Run, moon, moon, moon.
If the gypsies come,
they'll make necklaces, white rings
out of your heart.
Child, let me dance.
If the gypsies come
they'll find you on the anvil,*
your bright eyes closed.
Run, moon, moon, moon,
I hear their horses now.
Leave me, child, don't trample
my starched whiteness.

The horseman came nearer
drumming across the plain.
Inside the forge the child's
eyes are tight shut.
Through the olive-grove they came,
gypsies, bronze and sleep.
Heads high,
their eyes behind their lids.

How the barn-owl* sings,
how it sings in the tree!

Por el cielo va la luna
con un niño de la mano.

Dentro de la fragua lloran,
dando gritos, los gitanos.
El aire la vela, vela.
El aire la está velando.

Romance sonámbulo

A Gloria Giner y a Fernando de los Ríos

Verde que te quiero verde.
Verde viento. Verdes ramas.
El barco sobre la mar
y el caballo en la montaña.
Con la sombra en la cintura,
ella sueña en su baranda,
verde carne, pelo verde,
con ojos de fría plata.
Verde que te quiero verde.
Bajo la luna gitana,
las cosas la están mirando
y ella no puede mirarlas.

*

Verde que te quiero verde.
Grandes estrellas de escarcha
vienen con el pez de sombra
que abre el camino del alba.
La higuera frota su viento
con la lija de sus ramas,
y el monte, gato garduño,
eriza sus pitas agrias.
Pero ¿quién vendrá? ¿Y por dónde?...
Ella sigue en su baranda,
verde carne, pelo verde,
soñando en la mar amarga.

The moon goes through the sky
holding a child's hand.

Inside the forge the shouting
gypsies weep.
The air maintains its watch,
watching, watching.

Dreamwalker Ballad

To Gloria Giner and Fernando de los Ríos

Green how I want you green.
Green wind. Green branches.
Boat on the sea
and horse on the mountain.
Shadow at her waist
she dreams at her railing,
green flesh, green hair,
and eyes of cold silver.
Green how I want you green.
Beneath the gypsy moon
things are watching her
and she can't watch them.

*

Green how I want you green.
Great stars of frost,
arriving with the shadow-fish
that clears the way for dawn.
The fig-tree sandpapers
its wind on its branches,
and the mountain, like a thieving cat,
arches its back of sour agaves.
But who will come? And from where?...
She stays at the railing,
green flesh, green hair,
dreaming of the bitter sea.

*

—Compadre, quiero cambiar
mi caballo por su casa,
mi montura por su espejo,
mi cuchillo por su manta.
Compadre, vengo sangrando,
desde los puertos de Cabra.
—Si yo pudiera, mocito,
este trato se cerraba.
Pero yo ya no soy yo,
ni mi casa es ya mi casa.
—Compadre, quiero morir
decentemente en mi cama.
De acero, si puede ser,
con las sábanas de holanda.
¿No ves la herida que tengo
desde el pecho a la garganta?
—Trescientas rosas morenas
lleva tu pechera blanca.
Tu sangre rezuma y huele
alrededor de tu faja.
Pero yo ya no soy yo,
ni mi casa es ya mi casa.
—Dejadme subir al menos
hasta las altas barandas,
¡dejadme subir!, dejadme
hasta las verdes barandas.
Barandales de la luna
por donde retumba el agua.

*

Ya suben los dos compadres
hacia las altas barandas.
Dejando un rastro de sangre.
Dejando un rastro de lágrimas.
Temblaban en los tejados
farolillos de hojalata.
Mil panderos de cristal
herían la madrugada.

*

'Friend, I wish to trade
my horse for your house,
my saddle for your mirror,
my knife for your blanket.
Friend, I come bleeding
from the Cabra Pass.'
'If I could, young man,
I'd make you a deal.
But I'm not me any more,
my house is not my house.'
'Friend, I want to die
tucked up in my bed:
a steel bed, if possible,
with the finest linen sheets.
Don't you see this wound
from my chest to my throat?'
'Your white shirt sports
three hundred dark roses.
Your blood smells strong
oozing all around your sash.
But I'm not me any more,
my house is not my house.'
'At least let me climb
to the high railing,
let me climb, please,
up to the green rails!
Balustrades of the moon
where the water roars.'

*

And so the two friends climb
up to the high balustrade.
Leaving a trail of blood.
Leaving a trail of tears.
Little tin lanterns
trembled on the tiles.
A thousand crystal tambourines
wounded the dawning day.

*

Verde que te quiero verde,
verde viento, verdes ramas.
Los dos compadres subieron.
El largo viento, dejaba
en la boca un raro gusto
de hiel, de menta y de albahaca.
—¡Compadre! ¿Dónde está, dime,
dónde, está tu niña amarga?
—¡Cuántas veces te esperó!
¡Cuántas veces te esperara,
cara fresca, negro pelo,
en esta verde baranda!

*

Sobre el rostro del aljibe
se mecía la gitana.
Verde carne, pelo verde,
con ojos de fría plata.
Un carámbano de luna
la sostiene sobre el agua.
La noche se puso íntima
como una pequeña plaza.
Guardias civiles borrachos
en la puerta golpeaban.
Verde que te quiero verde.
Verde viento. Verdes ramas.
El barco sobre la mar.
Y el caballo en la montaña.

La monja gitana

A José Moreno Villa

Silencio de cal y mirto.
Malvas en las hierbas finas.
La monja borda alhelíes
sobre una tela pajiza.
Vuelan en la araña gris

*

Green how I want you green,
green wind, green branches.
The two friends climbed.
The long wind left
a strange taste in the mouth
of gall, mint, and basil.
'Friend, tell me, where is she,
where's your bitter girl?'
'The times she waited for you!
How often she would wait,
bright face, dark hair,
at this green railing!'

*

On the rain-well's face
the gypsy girl swayed.
Green flesh, green hair,
and eyes of cold silver.
An icicle of moonlight
holds her over the water.
The night became intimate
as a small town square.
Drunken Civil Guards*
beat at the door.
Green how I want you green.
Green wind. Green branches.
Boat on the sea.
And horse on the mountain.

The Gypsy Nun

To José Moreno Villa

Silence of myrtle and lime.
Wild mallow in fine grass.
The nun embroiders wallflowers
on a straw-coloured cloth.
The seven birds of the prism flit

siete pájaros del prisma.
La iglesia gruñe a lo lejos
como un oso panza arriba.
¡Qué bien borda! ¡Con qué gracia!
Sobre la tela pajiza,
ella quisiera bordar
flores de su fantasía.
¡Qué girasol! ¡Qué magnolia
de lentejuelas y cintas!
¡Qué azafranes y qué lunas,
en el mantel de la misa!
Cinco toronjas se endulzan
en la cercana cocina.
Las cinco llagas de Cristo
cortadas en Almería.
Por los ojos de la monja
galopan dos caballistas.
Un rumor último y sordo
le despega la camisa,
y al mirar nubes y montes
en las yertas lejanías,
se quiebra su corazón
de azúcar y yerbaluisa.
¡Oh, qué llanura empinada
con veinte soles arriba!
¡Qué ríos puestos de pie
vislumbra su fantasía!
Pero sigue con sus flores,
mientras que de pie, en la brisa,
la luz juega el ajedrez
alto de la celosía.

amongst the greyness of the chandelier.
The church growls in the distance
like a stricken bear.
How well she embroiders,
such finesse!
On the straw-yellow cloth
she'd like to embroider
flowers of her imagining.
What a sunflower! What a magnolia
of spangles and ribbons!
Such crocuses, such moons
on the altar cloth!
Five grapefruit sweeten
in the kitchen nearby.
Five nasturtiums,
the five wounds of Christ,*
cut in Almería.
Through the eyes of the nuns
two horsemen gallop.
A muffled far-off sound
lifts her petticoat,
and looking at the clouds and hills
in the distant wasteland,
her sugar and verbena heart breaks.
What an exalted plain
with twenty suns above!
What vertical rivers
her fantasy glimpses!
But she goes on with her flowers
while in the breeze
the tall light plays chess
with the window blinds.

Prendimiento de Antoñito el Camborio
en el camino de Sevilla

A Margarita Xirgu

Antonio Torres Heredia,
hijo y nieto de Camborios,
con una vara de mimbre
va a Sevilla a ver los toros.
Moreno de verde luna,
anda despacio y garboso.
Sus empavonados bucles
le brillan entre los ojos.
A la mitad del camino
cortó limones redondos,
y los fue tirando al agua
hasta que la puso de oro.
Y a la mitad del camino,
bajo las ramas de un olmo,
Guardia Civil caminera
lo llevó codo con codo.

*

El día se va despacio,
la tarde colgada a un hombro,
dando una larga torera
sobre el mar y los arroyos.
Las aceitunas aguardan
la noche de Capricornio,
y una corta brisa ecuestre
salta los montes de plomo.
Antonio Torres Heredia,
hijo y nieto de Camborios,
viene sin vara de mimbre
entre los cinco tricornios.

*

—Antonio, ¿quién eres tú?
Si te llamaras Camborio,
hubieras hecho una fuente ·

Capture of Antoñito el Camborio on the Seville Road

To Margarita Xirgu

Antonio Torres Heredia,
son and grandson of Camborios,
holding a willow-switch
is going to Seville to see the bulls.
Dark as a green moon
he walks. Unhurried. With style.
His curls' peacock sheen
glints between his eyes.
Midway through his journey
he cut some round lemons
and threw them one by one in the water
until it turned gold.
And midway through his journey
under the spread of an elm
a patrol of Civil Guard
grabbed him by the arm and led him off.

*

The day goes past slowly,
afternoon fastened at the shoulder,
a bullfighter's cape
passing over sea and rivulets.
The olives await
the Capricorn night,
and a snappy breeze jumps
the leaden hills like a horse.
Antonio Torres Heredia,
son and grandson of Camborios,
walks without his willow-switch
between the five three-cornered hats.

*

'Antonio, who are you?
Had your name been Camborio
you'd have made a fountain

de sangre con cinco chorros.
Ni tú eres hijo de nadie,
ni legítimo Camborio.
¡Se acabaron los gitanos
que iban por el monte solos!
Están los viejos cuchillos
tiritando bajo el polvo.

*

A las nueve de la noche
lo llevan al calabozo,
mientras los guardias civiles
beben limonada todos.
Y a las nueve de la noche
le cierran el calabozo,
mientras el cielo reluce
como la grupa de un potro.

Muerte de Antoñito el Camborio

A José Antonio Rubio Sacristán

Voces de muerte sonaron
cerca del Guadalquivir.
Voces antiguas que cercan
voz de clavel varonil.
Les clavó sobre las botas
mordiscos de jabalí.
En la lucha daba saltos
jabonados de delfín.
Bañó con sangre enemiga
su corbata carmesí,
pero eran cuatro puñales
y tuvo que sucumbir.
Cuando las estrellas clavan
rejones al agua gris,
cuando los erales sueñan
verónicas de alhelí,
voces de muerte sonaron
cerca del Guadalquivir.

of blood with five jets.
But you're the son of no one,
no true Camborio.
The gypsies have gone
who travelled the mountain alone.
Old knives shiver
beneath the dust.'

*

At nine in the evening
he's taken to a cell
while all the Civil Guards
drink lemonade.
And at nine in the evening
they lock his cell door,
while the sky gleams
like the flanks of a colt.

Death of Antoñito el Camborio

To José Antonio Rubio Sacristán

Voices of death sounded
by the Guadalquivir.
Ancient voices encircling
a virile carnation voice.
His boar's teeth
clamped themselves to their boots.
In the fight his leaps
were slippery as dolphins.
He soaked his crimson tie
in his enemy's blood
but there were four daggers
and he had to succumb.
When stars force lances
into grey water,
when novice bulls dream
of passes like wallflowers,
voices of death sounded
by the Guadalquivir.

*

—Antonio Torres Heredia,
Camborio de dura crin,
moreno de verde luna,
voz de clavel varonil:
¿quién te ha quitado la vida
cerca del Guadalquivir?
—Mis cuatro primos Heredias,
hijos de Benamejí.
Lo que en otros no envidiaban,
ya lo envidiaban en mí.
Zapatos color corinto,
medallones de marfil,
y este cutis amasado
con aceituna y jazmín.
—¡Ay Antonio el Camborio
digno de una Emperatriz!
Acuérdate de la Virgen
porque te vas a morir.
—¡Ay Federico García,
llama a la Guardia Civil!
Ya mi talle se ha quebrado
como caña de maíz.

*

Tres golpes de sangre tuvo,
y se murió de perfil.
Viva moneda que nunca
se volverá a repetir.
Un ángel marchoso pone
su cabeza en un cojín.
Otros de rubor cansado,
encendieron un candil.
Y cuando los cuatro primos
llegan a Benamejí,
voces de muerte cesaron
cerca del Guadalquivir.

*

'Antonio Torres Heredia,
tough-haired Camborio
dark as a green moon,
virile carnation voice.
Who's taken your life away
by the Guadalquivir?'
'My four Heredia cousins,
sons of Benamejí.
What they envied in no one
they envied in me.
My wine-coloured shoes,
my ivory medallions,
and my skin massaged
with olive and jasmine.'
'Oh, Antonio el Camborio,
worthy of an Empress!
Think of the Virgin
because you're going to die.'
'Oh, Federico García
call the Civil Guard!
My waist has snapped
like a stalk of maize.'

*

Three spurts of blood
and he died in profile.
A living coin which never
will be struck again.
A jaunty angel
lays his head on a cushion.
Others, weak blushes of colour,
light a lamp.
And when the four cousins
reach Benamejí
voices of death went silent
by the Guadalquivir.

Muerto de amor

A Margarita Manso

—¿Qué es aquello que reluce
por los altos corredores?
—Cierra la puerta, hijo mío,
acaban de dar las once.
—En mis ojos, sin querer,
relumbran cuatro faroles.
—Será que la gente aquella
estará fregando el cobre.

*

Ajo de agónica plata
la luna menguante, pone
cabelleras amarillas
a las amarillas torres.
La noche llama temblando
al cristal de los balcones
perseguida por los mil
perros que no la conocen,
y un olor de vino y ámbar
viene de los corredores.

*

Brisas de caña mojada
y rumor de viejas voces
resonaban por el arco
roto de la media noche.
Bueyes y rosas dormían.
Sólo por los corredores
las cuatro luces clamaban
con el furor de San Jorge.
Tristes mujeres del valle
bajaban su sangre de hombre,
tranquila de flor cortada
y amarga de muslo joven.
Viejas mujeres del río
lloraban al pie del monte,

Dead from Love

To Margarita Manso

'What is that gleaming
on the high galleries?'
'My son, close the door,
eleven has just struck.'
'Four unwelcome lamps
shine in my eyes.'
'The people there must be
scouring copperware.'

*

Garlic of dying silver
the waning moon places
heads of yellow hair
on the yellow towers.
Trembling night knocks
on the glass of the balconies
pursued by the thousand
dogs that don't know her,
and the smell of wine and amber
comes from the galleries.

*

Wet-reed breezes,
murmur of old voices
echoed through the round arch
of midnight.
Oxen and roses were sleeping.
Only four lights clamoured
in the galleries
raging like St George.*
Sad women of the valley
took down the blood of man,
still as a cut flower
and bitter as a young thigh.
Old women of the river
wept at the foot of the mountain,

un minuto intransitable
de cabelleras y nombres.
Fachadas de cal ponían
cuadrada y blanca la noche.
Serafines y gitanos
tocaban acordeones.
—Madre, cuando yo me muera
que se enteren los señores.
Pon telegramas azules
que vayan del Sur al Norte.

*

    Siete gritos, siete sangres,
siete adormideras dobles
quebraron opacas lunas
en los oscuros salones.
Lleno de manos cortadas
y coronitas de flores,
el mar de los juramentos
resonaba, no sé dónde.
Y el cielo daba portazos
al brusco rumor del bosque,
mientras clamaban las luces
en los altos corredores.

an impassable minute
of hair and names.
Façades of lime made
the night white and square.
Seraphs and gypsies
played accordions.
'Mother, when I die,
let the gentlemen know.
Send azure telegrams*
from South to North.'

                    *

Seven shouts, seven bloods,
seven double poppies
smashed opaque moons
in the darkened rooms.
Full of cut hands
and coronets of flowers,
the sea of oaths
echoed who knows where.
And the sky slammed its door
on the sudden noise of the wood,
while lights clamoured
in the high galleries.

Poemas de *Poeta en Nueva York*

El rey de Harlem

Con una cuchara
arrancaba los ojos a los cocodrilos
y golpeaba el trasero de los monos.
Con una cuchara.

Fuego de siempre dormía en los pedernales
y los escarabajos borrachos de anís
olvidaban el musgo de las aldeas.
Aquel viejo cubierto de setas
iba al sitio donde lloraban los negros
mientras crujía la cuchara del rey
y llegaban los tanques de agua podrida.

Las rosas huían por los filos
de las últimas curvas del aire,
y en los montones de azafrán
los niños machacaban pequeñas ardillas
con un rubor de frenesí manchado.

Es preciso cruzar los puentes
y llegar al rumor negro
para que el perfume de pulmón
nos golpee las sienes con su vestido
de caliente piña.

Es preciso matar al rubio vendedor de aguardiente,
a todos los amigos de la manzana y de la arena;
y es necesario dar con los puños cerrados
a las pequeñas judías que tiemblan llenas de burbujas,
para que el rey de Harlem cante con su muchedumbre,
para que los cocodrilos duerman en largas filas
bajo el amianto de la luna,
y para que nadie dude la infinita belleza
de los plumeros, los ralladores, los cobres y las cacerolas de las cocinas.

From *Poet in New York*

The King of Harlem

With a spoon
he scooped out crocodiles' eyes
and whacked monkeys' backsides.
With a spoon.

The fire of forever slept in the flints
and beetles drunk on anis
forgot the village moss.
The old mushroom-covered man
went to where the blacks wept
while the king's spoon crackled
and tanks of putrid water arrived.

Roses fled along the ridge
of air's last curves
and on the mounds of saffron
children squashed little squirrels
flushing red in tainted frenzy.

You have to cross the bridges
and reach the black murmur
so that the scent of lungs
hits your temples, dressed
in warm pineapple.

You must kill the blond-haired brandy-seller
and every friend of sand and apple
and with clenched fists you must beat
the trembling little Jewish women full of bubbles
so the king of Harlem may sing with his throng,
the crocodiles sleep in long rows
beneath the moon's asbestos,
and no one doubt the infinite beauty
of dusters, graters, copperware, kitchen pans.

¡Ay, Harlem! ¡Ay, Harlem! ¡Ay, Harlem!
No hay angustia comparable a tus rojos oprimidos,
a tu sangre estremecida dentro del eclipse oscuro,
a tu violencia granate, sordomuda en la penumbra,
a tu gran rey prisionero, con un traje de conserje.

*

Tenía la noche una hendidura y quietas salamandras de marfil.
Las muchachas americanas
llevaban niños y monedas en el vientre
y los muchachos se desmayaban en la cruz del desperezo.

Ellos son.
Ellos son los que beben el whisky de plata junto a los volcanes
y tragan pedacitos de corazón por las heladas montañas del oso.

*

Aquella noche el rey de Harlem, con una durísima cuchara,
arrancaba los ojos a los cocodrilos
y golpeaba el trasero de los monos.
Con una cuchara.

Los negros lloraban confundidos
entre paraguas y soles de oro,
los mulatos estiraban gomas, ansiosos de llegar al torso blanco,
y el viento empañaba espejos
y quebraba las venas de los bailarines.

Negros, Negros, Negros, Negros,

la sangre no tiene puertas en vuestra noche boca arriba.
No hay rubor. Sangre furiosa por debajo de las pieles.
Viva en la espina del puñal y en el pecho de los paisajes,
bajo las pinzas y las retamas de la celeste luna de cáncer.

Sangre que busca por mil caminos muertes enharinadas y ceniza de
    nardo,
cielos yertos, en declive, donde las colonias de planetas
rueden por las playas con los objetos abandonados.

Ay Harlem, Harlem, Harlem!
There's no anguish like your oppressed reds,
or the shudder of your blood within the dark eclipse,
or your garnet violence, deaf and dumb in the shadows,
or your great king held captive in a commissioner's coat.

*

The night was rent, and there were silent ivory salamanders.
American girls
carried children and coins in their bellies
and boys fainted racked on the cross.

They.
They who drink silver whisky by volcanoes
and swallow little pieces of heart on the frozen mountains of the bear.

*

That night the king of Harlem with an indestructible spoon
scooped out crocodiles' eyes
and whacked monkeys' backsides.
With a spoon.

Blacks wept confounded
among golden suns and umbrellas,
mulattos stretched rubber, keen to get to white torsos,
and the wind clouded mirrors
and broke the dancers' veins.

Blacks, blacks, blacks, blacks.

Blood has no doors in your night on its back.
No flush. Bad blood beneath the skin,
alert in the dagger's thorn and the landscapes' heart,
under the pincers and the Spanish broom of Cancer's celestial moon.

Blood searching a thousand highways for flour-sprinkled deaths,
    spikenard ash,
rigid angled skies where colonies of planets
can roll along beaches with the jetsam.

Sangre que mira lenta con el rabo del ojo,
hecha de espartos exprimidos, néctares de subterráneos.
Sangre que oxida al alisio descuidado en una huella
y disuelve a las mariposas en los cristales de la ventana.

Es la sangre que viene, que vendrá
por los tejados y azoteas, por todas partes,
para quemar la clorofila de las mujeres rubias,
para gemir al pie de las camas, ante el insomnio de los lavabos,
y estrellarse en una aurora de tabaco y bajo amarillo.

¡Hay que huir!,
huir por las esquinas y encerrarse en los últimos pisos,
porque el tuétano del bosque penetrará por las rendijas
para dejar en vuestra carne una leve huella de eclipse
y una falsa tristeza de guante desteñido y rosa química.

                              *

Es por el silencio sapientísimo
cuando los camareros y los cocineros y los que limpian con la lengua
las heridas de los millonarios
buscan al rey por las calles o en los ángulos del salitre.

Un viento sur de madera, oblicuo en el negro fango,
escupe a las barcas rotas y se clava puntillas en los hombros.
Un viento sur que lleva
colmillos, girasoles, alfabetos
y una pila de Volta con avispas ahogadas.

El olvido estaba expresado por tres gotas de tinta sobre el monóculo.
El amor, por un solo rostro invisible a flor de piedra.
Médulas y corolas componían sobre las nubes
un desierto de tallos, sin una sola rosa.

                              *

A la izquierda, a la derecha, por el Sur y por el Norte,
se levanta el muro impasible
para el topo y la aguja del agua.
No busquéis, negros, su grieta

Blood looking askance, slow,
made of dried esparto, underground nectars.
Blood that oxidizes the careless trade wind in a footprint,
and dissolves butterflies on window-panes.

It's the blood that comes, that will come
over roofs and terraces, from everywhere,
to burn the chlorophyll of fair-haired women,
to moan at the foot of beds before the insomnia of basins
and smash against a yellow-bile tobacco dawn.

Flee,
you must flee round corners, lock yourself on top floors,
because the pith of the forest will come through cracks
to leave on your flesh the faint trace of an eclipse
and the false sadness of discoloured glove and chemical rose.

*

It's in this wisest silence
that waiters, cooks, and tongues that clean
the wounds of millionaires
search the streets and saltpetre corners for the king.

A south wind of wood, slanting through black mud,
spits at broken boats, drives nails in its shoulders,
a south wind that carries
alphabets, sunflowers, tusks
and a battery with drowned wasps.

Oblivion was expressed in three drops of ink on the monocle.
Love, in one invisible face on the surface of the stone.
Marrow and corollas on the clouds formed
a desert of stalks without a single rose.

*

To the left, to the right, south and north,
the wall rises impervious
to mole or spike of water.
Don't search, blacks, for a breach

para hallar la máscara infinita.
Buscar el gran sol del centro
hechos una piña zumbadora.
El sol que se desliza por los bosques
seguro de no encontrar una ninfa.
El sol que destruye números y no ha cruzado nunca un sueño,
el tatuado sol que baja por el río
y muge seguido de caimanes.

Negros, Negros, Negros, Negros,

Jamás sierpe ni cebra ni mula
palidecieron al morir.
El leñador no sabe cuándo expiran
los clamorosos árboles que corta.
Aguardad bajo la sombra vegetal de vuestro rey
a que cicutas y cardos y ortigas turben postreras azoteas.

Entonces, negros, entonces, entonces,
podréis besar con frenesí las ruedas de las bicicletas,
poner parejas de microscopios en las cuevas de las ardillas
y danzar al fin sin duda, mientras las flores erizadas
asesinan a nuestro Moisés casi en los juncos del cielo.

¡Ay, Harlem disfrazada!
¡Ay, Harlem, amenazada por un gentío de trajes sin cabeza!
Me llega tu rumor,
me llega tu rumor atravesando troncos y ascensores,
a través de láminas grises,
donde flotan tus automóviles cubiertos de dientes,
a través de los caballos muertos y los crímenes diminutos,
a través de tu gran rey desesperado,
cuyas barbas llegan al mar.

Crucifixión

La luna pudo detenerse al fin por la curva blanquísima de los
　　caballos
Un rayo de luz violenta que se escapaba de la herida
proyectó en el cielo el instante de la circuncisión de un niño muerto.

where you might find the infinite mask.
Turn into a buzzing pineapple,
seek the great central sun.
The sun that glides through the woods
certain it won't meet a nymph,
the sun that kills numbers, that's never met a dream,
tattooed sun, moving downriver, bellowing,
with alligators in pursuit.

Blacks, blacks, blacks, blacks.

Never did snake, zebra, mule
grow pale at death.
The woodcutter doesn't know when
the clamouring trees he cuts expire.
Wait in the leafy shadow of your king
until hemlock and thistle and nettles disturb the furthest terrace roots.

Then blacks, then, then
you can plant frenzied kisses on bicycle wheels,
put pairs of microscopes in squirrels' nests,
and dance at last with confidence, while bristling flowers
mow down our Moses close to the reeds of heaven.

Ay, Harlem in disguise!
Ay Harlem, threatened by a gang of headless costumes!
Your murmur reaches me
through tree-trunks and lifts,
through sheets of grey metal
where your cars float bristling with teeth,
through dead horses and petty crimes,
through your great despairing king
whose beard reaches the sea.

Crucifixion

In the end the moon could stay on the horses' blinding white
   curve.
A ray of violent light escaping from the wound
shot the instant of a dead boy's circumcision into the sky.

La sangre bajaba por el monte y los ángeles la buscaban,
pero los cálices eran de viento y al fin llenaba los zapatos.
Cojos perros fumaban sus pipas y un olor de cuero caliente
ponía grises los labios redondos de los que vomitaban en las
　　esquinas.
Y llegaban largos alaridos por el Sur de la noche seca.
Era que la luna quemaba con sus bujías el falo de los caballos.
Un sastre especialista en púrpura
había encerrado a las tres santas mujeres
y les enseñaba una calavera por vidrios de la ventana.
Los niños en el arrabal rodeaban a un camello blanco
que lloraba asustado porque al alba
tenía que pasar sin remedio por el ojo de una aguja.
¡Oh cruz! ¡Oh clavos! ¡Oh espina!
¡Oh espina clavada en el hueso hasta que se oxiden los planetas!
Como nadie volvía la cabeza, el cielo pudo desnudarse.
Entonces se oyó la gran voz y los fariseos dijeron:
«Esa maldita vaca tiene las tetas llenas de leche.»
La muchedumbre cerraba las puertas
y la lluvia bajaba por las calles decidida a mojar el corazón
mientras la tarde se puso turbia de latidos y leñadores
y la oscura ciudad agonizaba bajo el martillo de los carpinteros.
«Esa maldita vaca
tiene las tetas llenas de perdigones»,
dijeron los fariseos.
Pero la sangre mojó sus pies y los espíritus inmundos
estrellaban ampollas de laguna sobre las paredes del templo.
Se supo el momento preciso de la salvación de nuestra vida.
Porque la luna lavó con agua
las quemaduras de los caballos
y no la primera vida que callaron en la arena.
Entonces salieron los fríos cantando sus canciones
y las ranas encendieron sus lumbres en la doble orilla del río.
«Esa maldita vaca, maldita, maldita, maldita,
no nos dejará dormir», dijeron los fariseos,
y se alejaron a sus casas por el tumulto de la calle
dando empujones a los borrachos y escupiendo la sal de los
　　sacrificios
mientras la sangre los seguía con un balido de cordero.

Blood flowed down the mountain and the angels searched it out,
but the chalices were wind and eventually filled the shoes.
Lame dogs smoked pipes and the smell of hot leather
turned the fat lips of people vomiting in corners grey.
And long shrieks came from the South of dry night—
the moon's candles were burning the horses' phalluses.
A tailor who specialized in purple
had shut three saintly ladies in
and was showing them a skull through his window.
At the edge of the town, kids surrounded a white camel
weeping because at dawn it would have
to pass through the eye of a needle.
O cross! Nails! Thorn!
Thorn driven into bone until planets rust!
As no one was spying the sky could undress.
Then the huge voice was heard and the Pharisees said:
'This wretched cow's teats are bursting with milk.'
The crowd closed its doors
and the rain poured down the streets bent on soaking hearts
while evening turned cloudy with beats and woodcutters
and the dark city lay dying under the carpenters' hammers.
'The teats of this wretched cow
are stuffed with bird-shot'
said the Pharisees.
But blood soaked their feet and filthy spirits
spangled lake-bubbles over the temple walls.
The precise moment of saving our life became known.
Because the moon washed with water
the horses' burns,
not the first life they silenced in the sand.
Then cold emerged singing its various songs
and frogs lit their lamps on the river's double banks.
'This wretched cow, three times cursed,
won't let us sleep', said the Pharisees,
and they left for home through turbulent streets,
jostling drunks and spitting the salt of sacrifice,
while blood followed them bleating like a lamb.

Fue entonces
y la tierra despertó arrojando temblorosos ríos de polilla.

Grito hacia Roma

(Desde la torre del Chrysler Building)

Manzanas levemente heridas
por finos espadines de plata,
nubes rasgadas por una mano de coral
que lleva en el dorso una almendra de fuego,
peces de arsénico como tiburones,
tiburones como gotas de llanto para cegar una multitud,
rosas que hieren
y agujas instaladas en los caños de la sangre,
mundos enemigos y amores cubiertos de gusanos
caerán sobre ti. Caerán sobre la gran cúpula
que unta de aceite las lenguas militares,
donde un hombre se orina en una deslumbrante paloma
y escupe carbón machacado
rodeado de miles de campanillas.

Porque ya no hay quien reparta el pan y el vino,
ni quien cultive hierbas en la boca del muerto,
ni quien abra los linos del reposo,
ni quien llore por las heridas de los elefantes.
No hay más que un millón de herreros
forjando cadenas para los niños que han de venir.
No hay más que un millón de carpinteros
que hacen ataúdes sin cruz.
No hay más que un gentío de lamentos
que se abren las ropas en espera de la bala.
El hombre que desprecia la paloma debía hablar,
debía gritar desnudo entre las columnas
y ponerse una inyección para adquirir la lepra
y llorar un llanto tan terrible
que disolviera sus anillos y sus teléfonos de diamante.
Pero el hombre vestido de blanco
ignora el misterio de la espiga,

That was then,
and the world awoke launching tremulous rivers of moths.

Cry to Rome

(From the Tower of the Chrysler Building)

Apples with flesh-wounds
made by slender silver swords,
clouds slashed by a coral hand,
a fire-filled almond on its back,
arsenic fish like sharks,
sharks like tear-drops to blind a multitude,
roses that wound
and needles lodged in the blood's tubes,
enemy worlds and worm-covered loves
will fall on you. On the great dome
that anoints military tongues with olive oil
where a man pisses on a luminous dove
and spits crushed coal
ringed by a thousand little bells.

Because now there's no one to share the bread and wine,
or grow grass in the dead man's mouth,
or unfold the linen of repose,
or to grieve over elephant wounds.
Just a million blacksmiths
forging chains for children yet unborn.
Just a million carpenters
making coffins without crosses.
Just a throng of lamentations
opening their clothes, awaiting the bullet.
The man who despises the dove should have spoken,
yelled, naked among columns,
injected himself with leprosy,
and set up a wail so dreadful
it dissolved his rings and diamond telephones.
But the man dressed in white*
knows nothing of the mystery of corn,

ignora el gemido de la parturienta,
ignora que Cristo puede dar agua todavía,
ignora que la moneda quema el beso de prodigio
y da la sangre del cordero al pico idiota del faisán.

Los maestros enseñan a los niños
una luz maravillosa que viene del monte;
pero lo que llega es una reunión de cloacas
donde gritan las oscuras ninfas del cólera.
Los maestros señalan con devoción las enormes cúpulas sahumadas;
pero debajo de las estatuas no hay amor,
no hay amor bajo los ojos de cristal definitivo.
El amor está en las carnes desgarradas por la sed,
en la choza diminuta que lucha con la inundación;
el amor está en los fosos donde luchan las sierpes del hambre,
en el triste mar que mece los cadáveres de las gaviotas
y en el oscurísimo beso punzante debajo de las almohadas.

Pero el viejo de las manos traslúcidas
dirá: amor, amor, amor,
aclamado por millones de moribundos;
dirá: amor, amor, amor,
entre el tisú estremecido de ternura;
dirá: paz, paz, paz,
entre el tirite de cuchillos y melones de dinamita;
dirá: amor, amor, amor,
hasta que se le pongan de plata los labios.

Mientras tanto, mientras tanto, ¡ay!, mientras tanto,
los negros que sacan las escupideras,
los muchachos que tiemblan bajo el terror pálido de los directores,
las mujeres ahogadas en aceites minerales,
la muchedumbre de martillo, de violín o de nube,
ha de gritar aunque le estrellen los sesos en el muro,
ha de gritar frente a las cúpulas,
ha de gritar loca de fuego,
ha de gritar loca de nieve,
ha de gritar con la cabeza llena de excremento,

knows nothing of the cries of a woman in labour,
doesn't know that Christ can still give water,
doesn't know that money burns the prodigy's kiss
and gives lamb's blood to the pheasant's idiot beak.

The teachers show the children
a marvellous light coming from the mountain;
but what arrives is a union of sewers
where the dark nymphs of cholera scream.
Devoutly the teachers point out huge fumigated domes;
but beneath the statues there's no love,
no love beneath the eyes set in crystal.
Love is there, in flesh ripped by thirst,
in the tiny hut struggling against the flood;
love is there, in ditches where snakes of hunger wrestle,
in the sad sea that rocks dead gulls,
and in the darkest stinging kiss under pillows.

But the old man with the luminous hands
will say: love, love, love,
cheered on by millions of the dying;
will say: love, love, love,
in the shimmering tissue of tenderness:
will say: peace, peace, peace,
among shivering knives and melons of dynamite;
will say: love, love, love,
until his lips turn to silver.

Meanwhile and meanwhile and meanwhile,
blacks collecting up the spittoons,
boys trembling beneath directors' bloodless ferocity,
women drowned in mineral oils,
crowd with hammer, violin or cloud
must yell even if their brains splatter on the wall,
yell before the domes,
yell maddened by fire,
yell maddened by snow,
yell with heads full of excrement,

ha de gritar como todas las noches juntas,
ha de gritar con voz tan desgarrada
hasta que las ciudades tiemblen como niñas
y rompan las prisiones del aceite y la música.
Porque queremos el pan nuestro de cada día,
flor de aliso y perenne ternura desgranada,
porque queremos que se cumpla la voluntad de la Tierra
que da sus frutos para todos.

Son de negros en Cuba

Cuando llegue la luna llena iré a Santiago de Cuba,
iré a Santiago
en un coche de agua negra.
Iré a Santiago.
Cantarán los techos de palmera.
Iré a Santiago.
Cuando la palma quiere ser cigüeña,
iré a Santiago.
Y cuando quiere ser medusa el plátano,
iré a Santiago.
Iré a Santiago
con la rubia cabeza de Fonseca.
Iré a Santiago.
Y con el rosa de Romeo y Julieta
iré a Santiago.
Mar de papel y plata de moneda.
Iré a Santiago.
¡Oh Cuba! ¡Oh ritmo de semillas secas!
Iré a Santiago.
¡Oh cintura caliente y gota de madera!
Iré a Santiago.
Arpa de troncos vivos. Caimán. Flor de tabaco.
Iré a Santiago.
Siempre he dicho que yo iría a Santiago
en un coche de agua negra.
Iré a Santiago.
Brisa y alcohol en las ruedas,

yell like every night in one,
yell with a voice torn terribly
until cities tremble like girls
and burst the prisons of oil and music,
because we want our daily bread,
alder-flower and everlasting harvest of tenderness,
because we want Earth's will be done,
the Earth that gives her fruit to all.

Blacks in Cuba, Their *Son*

As soon as there's a full moon, I'll go to Santiago, Cuba,
I'll go to Santiago
in a coach of black water.
I'll go to Santiago.
Palm roofs will sing.
I'll go to Santiago.
When the palm tree wants to be a stork,
I'll go to Santiago.
And when the banana tree wants to be a jellyfish,
I'll go to Santiago.
I'll go to Santiago
with Fonseca's fair head.
I'll go to Santiago.
And with Romeo and Juliet's* rose
I'll go to Santiago.
Paper sea, silver coins.
I'll go to Santiago.
O Cuba, rhythm of dried seeds!
I'll go to Santiago.
Torrid waist, drop of wood!
I'll go to Santiago.
Harp of living trunks, alligator, tobacco flower!
I'll go to Santiago.
I always said I'd go to Santiago
in a coach of black water.
I'll go to Santiago.
Breeze and alcohol in the wheels,

iré a Santiago.
Mi coral en la tiniebla,
iré a Santiago.
El mar ahogado en la arena,
iré a Santiago.
Calor blanco, fruta muerta,
iré a Santiago.
¡Oh bovino frescor de cañavera!
¡Oh Cuba! ¡Oh curva de suspiro y barro!
Iré a Santiago.

I'll go to Santiago.
My coral in the darkness,
I'll go to Santiago.
Sea buried in sand.
I'll go to Santiago.
White heat, dead fruit,
I'll go to Santiago.
Bovine freshness of sugar cane!
O Cuba! Curve of sigh and clay!
I'll go to Santiago.

Poema de *Tierra y Luna*

Pequeño poema infinito

Para Luis Cardoza y Aragón

Equivocar el camino
es llegar a la nieve
y llegar a la nieve
es pacer durante varios siglos las hierbas de los cementerios.

Equivocar el camino
es llegar a la mujer,
la mujer que no teme la luz,
la mujer que mata dos gallos en un segundo,
la luz que no teme a los gallos
y los gallos que no saben cantar sobre la nieve.

Pero si la nieve se equivoca de corazón
puede llegar el viento Austro,
y como el aire no hace caso de los gemidos,
tendremos que pacer otra vez las hierbas de los cementerios.
Yo vi dos dolorosas espigas de cera
que enterraban un paisaje de volcanes
y vi dos niños locos
que empujaban llorando las pupilas de un asesino.

Pero el dos no ha sido nunca un número
porque es una angustia y su sombra,
porque es la demostración del otro infinito que no es suyo
y es las murallas del muerto
y el castigo de la nueva resurrección sin finales.

Los muertos odian el número dos,
pero el número dos adormece a las mujeres,
y como la mujer teme la luz,
la luz tiembla delante de los gallos
y los gallos sólo saben volar sobre la nieve,
tendremos que pacer sin descanso las hierbas de los cementerios.

From *Earth and Moon*

Little Infinite Poem

For Luis Cardoza y Aragón

To take the wrong road
is to arrive at snow
and arriving at snow
is to graze for centuries on graveyard weeds.

To take the wrong road
is to arrive at woman,
woman fearless of light,
woman who kills two cockerels in a flash,
light which doesn't fear cockerels
and cockerels that can't crow on snow.

But if snow gets the wrong heart
the South Wind may come,
and since air pays moans no heed,
we'll have to graze on graveyard weeds again.
I saw two sorrowing wax spikes of wheat
burying a volcanic landscape,
and two mad weeping children
pushing a murderer's eyeballs.

But two has never been a number;
it is anguish and its shadow,
the demonstration of another's infinity,
the dead man's ramparts
and the punishment of new and endless resurrection.

Dead men hate the number two,
but that number lulls women to sleep,
and as woman fears light,
and light trembles before cockerels,
and cockerels can only fly above the snow,
we'll have to graze for good on graveyard weeds.

Poemas de *Diván del Tamarit*

Gacela IX
Del amor maravilloso

Con todo el yeso
de los malos campos,
eras junco de amor, jazmín mojado.

Con sur y llama
de los malos cielos,
eras rumor de nieve por mi pecho.

Cielos y campos
anudaban cadenas en mis manos.

Campos y cielos
azotaban las llagas de mi cuerpo.

Casida V
Del sueño al aire libre

Flor de jazmín y toro degollado.
Pavimento infinito. Mapa. Sala. Arpa. Alba.
La niña sueña un toro de jazmines
y el toro es un sangriento crepúsculo que brama.

Si el cielo fuera un niño pequeñito,
los jazmines tendrían mitad de noche oscura,
y el toro circo azul sin lidiadores,
y un corazón al pie de una columna.

Pero el cielo es un elefante,
el jazmín es un agua sin sangre,
y la niña es un ramo nocturno
por el inmenso pavimento oscuro.

From *The Tamarit Divan*

Ghazal IX
Of Marvellous Love

With all the gypsum
of the badlands,
you were reed of love, moist jasmine.

With south and fire
of the bad skies,
you were murmur of snow in my breast.

Skies and fields
knotted chains in my hands.

Fields and skies
scourged the wounds in my flesh.

Qasida V
Of the Open-Air Dream

Jasmine bloom and butchered bull.
Endless paving. Map. Room. Harp. Dawn.
The girl feigns a jasmine bull
and the bull's a bleeding sunset, bellowing.

If the sky were a tiny child,
half the jasmines' night would be darkness,
the bull a blue arena without matadors,
and a heart at the foot of a column.

But the sky's an elephant,
and jasmine bloodless water.
The girl's a bough by night
on the huge dark paving.

Entre el jazmín y el toro
o garfios de marfil o gente dormida.
En el jazmín un elefante y nubes
y en el toro el esqueleto de la niña.

Casida VIII
De la muchacha dorada

La muchacha dorada
se bañaba en el agua
y el agua se doraba.

Las algas y las ramas
en sombra la asombraban,
y el ruiseñor cantaba
por la muchacha blanca.

Vino la noche clara,
turbia de plata mala,
con peladas montañas
bajo la brisa parda.

La muchacha mojada
era blanca en el agua
y el agua, llamarada.

Vino el alba sin mancha,
con cien caras de vaca,
yerta y amortajada
con heladas guirnaldas.

La muchacha de lágrimas
se bañaba entre llamas,
y el ruiseñor lloraba
con las alas quemadas.

La muchacha dorada
era una blanca garza
y el agua la doraba.

Between the bull and the jasmine
either marble claws or people sleeping.
In the jasmine, an elephant and clouds
and in the bull the girl's skeleton.

Qasida VIII
Of the Golden Girl

The golden girl
bathed in the water
and the water turned gold.

Algae and branches
darkened her with shadows,
and the nightingale sang
for the white girl.

The clear night came
clouded with bad silver,
bringing bald mountains
under the cloudy breeze.

The drenched girl
was white in the water
and the water a splash.

The spotless dawn arrived,
with its faces of a thousand cows,
rigid and laid out
with frozen garlands.

The girl of tears
bathed among flames
and the nightingale wept,
wings burnt.

The golden girl
was a white heron,
and the water made it gold.

Gacela del mercado matutino

Por el arco de Elvira
quiero verte pasar,
para saber tu nombre
y ponerme a llorar.

¿Qué luna gris de las nueve
te desangró la mejilla?
¿Quién recoge tu semilla
de llamarada en la nieve?
¿Qué alfiler de cactus breve
asesina tu cristal?…

Por el arco de Elvira
voy a verte pasar,
para beber tus ojos
y ponerme a llorar.

¡Qué voz para mi castigo
levantas por el mercado!
¡Qué clavel enajenado
en los montones de trigo!
¡Qué lejos estoy contigo,
qué cerca cuando te vas!

Por el arco de Elvira
voy a verte pasar,
para sentir tus muslos
y ponerme a llorar.

Ghazal of the Morning Marketplace

Through Elvira's Arch*
I want to see you pass,
find out your name
and start to cry.

What grey nine o'clock moon
drained your cheek of blood?
Who gathers up your seed,
sudden splash on the snow?
What needle of brief cactus
assassinates your crystal?...

Through Elvira's Arch
I'm going to see you pass,
drink your eyes
and start to cry.

Your voice raised to punish me
in the marketplace!
The carnation exiled
in the wheat-piles!
How distant, you and I together,
how close when you depart!

Through Elvira's Arch
I'm going to see you pass,
know your thighs
and start to cry.

Poemas de *Seis Poemas Galegos*

Romaxe de Nosa Señora da Barca

¡Ay ruada, ruada, ruada
da Virxe pequena
e a súa barca!

A Virxe era de pedra
e a súa coroa de prata.
Marelos os catro bois
que no seu carro a levaban.

Pombas de vidro traguían
a choiva pol-a montana.
Mortos e mortas de néboa
pol-os sendeiros chegaban.

¡Virxe, deixa a túa cariña
nos doces ollos das vacas
e leva sobr'o teu manto
as froles da amortallada!

Pol-a testa de Galicia
xa ven salaiando a i-alba.
A Virxe mira pr'o mar
dend'a porta da súa casa.

¡Ay ruada, ruada, ruada
da Virxe pequena
e a súa barca!

Canzón de cuna pra Rosalía Castro, morta

¡Érguete, miña amiga,
que xa cantan os galos do día!
¡Érguete, miña amada,
porque o vento muxe coma unha vaca!

From *Six Galician Poems*

Romance of Our Lady of the Boat

Pilgrimage, pilgrimage!
Pilgrimage to the little Virgin
and her boat!

The Virgin was stone,
her crown silver.
Four ochre oxen
carrying her in their cart.

Crystal doves brought rain
over the mountain.
Misty dead arrived,
came down the paths.

Virgin, leave your sweet face
in the cows' soft eyes,
and wear on your robe
the flowers of death's shroud!

Here's shivering dawn,
rounding the tip of Galicia.
From her doorway
the Virgin looks to the sea.

Pilgrimage, pilgrimage!
Pilgrimage to the little Virgin
and her boat!

Cradle Song for Rosalía Castro, Dead

Rise, sweet friend,
cockerels sing the dawn!
Rise, sweet love,
the wind lows like a cow!

Os arados van e vên
dende Santiago a Belén.
Dende Belén a Santiago
un anxo ven en un barco.
Un barco de prata fina
que trai a door de Galicia.
Galicia deitada e queda,
transida de tristes herbas.
Herbas que cobren teu leito
e a negra fonte dos teus cabelos.
Cabelos que van ô mar
onde as nubens teñen seu nidio pombal.

¡Érguete, miña amiga,
que xa cantan os galos do día!
¡Érguete, miña amada,
porque o vento muxe como unha vaca!

The ploughs go back and forth
from Santiago* to Bethlehem.
From Santiago to Bethlehem
an angel comes in a boat.
A boat of fine silver
bearing Galicia's grief.
Silent Galicia stretched out,
worn with sad weeds,
weeds that cover your bed,
and the dark fountain of your hair.
Hair that goes to the sea
with its bright dovecote of clouds.

Rise, sweet friend,
cockerels sing the dawn!
Rise, sweet love,
the wind lows like a cow!

Llanto por Ignacio Sánchez Mejías

A mi querida amiga Encarnación López Júlvez

1. La cogida y la muerte

A las cinco de la tarde.
Eran las cinco en punto de la tarde.
Un niño trajo la blanca sábana
a las cinco de la tarde.
Una espuerta de cal ya prevenida
a las cinco de la tarde.
Lo demás era muerte y sólo muerte
a las cinco de la tarde.

El viento se llevó los algodones
a las cinco de la tarde.
Y el óxido sembró cristal y níquel
a las cinco de la tarde.
Ya luchan la paloma y el leopardo
a las cinco de la tarde.
Y un muslo con un asta desolada
a las cinco de la tarde.
Comenzaron los sones de bordón
a las cinco de la tarde.
Las campanas de arsénico y el humo
a las cinco de la tarde.
En las esquinas grupos de silencio
a las cinco de la tarde.
¡Y el toro solo corazón arriba!
a las cinco de la tarde.
Cuando el sudor de nieve fue llegando
a las cinco de la tarde,
cuando la plaza se cubrió de yodo
a las cinco de la tarde,
la muerte puso huevos en la herida
a las cinco de la tarde.

Lament for Ignacio Sánchez Mejías

To my dear friend Encarnación López Júlvez

1. Goring and Death

At five in the afternoon.
Five on the dot after noon.
A boy fetched the white sheet
at five in the afternoon.
A basket of lime waiting
at five in the afternoon.
After that death and only death
at five in the afternoon.

The wind blew cotton scraps
at five in the afternoon.
And oxide sowed crystal and nickel
at five in the afternoon.
Dove and leopard battle
at five in the afternoon.
A thigh with a desolate horn
at five in the afternoon.
The bass drone began
at five in the afternoon.
Arsenic bells and smoke
at five in the afternoon.
On corners groups of silence
at five in the afternoon.
And the bull alone elated*
at five in the afternoon.
When sweats of snow began
at five in the afternoon.
And iodine covered the ring
at five in the afternoon.
Death laid its eggs in the wound
at five in the afternoon.

A las cinco de la tarde.
A las cinco en punto de la tarde.

Un ataúd con ruedas es la cama
a las cinco de la tarde.
Huesos y flautas suenan en su oído
a las cinco de la tarde.
El toro ya mugía por su frente
a las cinco de la tarde.
El cuarto se irisaba de agonía
a las cinco de la tarde.
A lo lejos ya viene la gangrena
a las cinco de la tarde.
Trompa de lirio por las verdes ingles
a las cinco de la tarde.
Las heridas quemaban como soles
a las cinco de la tarde,
y el gentío rompía las ventanas
a las cinco de la tarde.
A las cinco de la tarde.
¡Ay qué terribles cinco de la tarde!
¡Eran las cinco en todos los relojes!
¡Eran las cinco en sombra de la tarde!

2. La sangre derramada

¡Que no quiero verla!

Dile a la luna que venga,
que no quiero ver la sangre
de Ignacio sobre la arena.

¡Que no quiero verla!

La luna de par en par,
caballo de nubes quietas,
y la plaza gris del sueño
con sauces en las barreras.

At five in the afternoon.
At five on the dot after noon.

A coffin on wheels is the bed
at five in the afternoon.
Bones and flutes sound in his ear
at five in the afternoon.
In his face the bull's bellowing
at five in the afternoon.
The rainbow of death entered the room
at five in the afternoon.
Far off, gangrene on its way
at five in the afternoon.
Lily-trumpet in the green groin
at five in the afternoon.
The wounds burned like suns
at five in the afternoon,
and the crowd smashed the windows
at five in the afternoon.
At five in the afternoon.
Terrible five after noon!
Every clock pointing to five!
Five after noon in the shade!

2. Spilled Blood

I will not see it!

Tell the moon to come,
I will not see the blood
of Ignacio on the sand.

I will not see it!

The moon wide-open.
A horse of quiet clouds
And dream's grey bull-ring
edged all round with willows.

¡Que no quiero verla!
Que mi recuerdo se quema.
¡Avisad a los jazmines
con su blancura pequeña!

¡Que no quiero verla!

La vaca del viejo mundo
pasaba su triste lengua
sobre un hocico de sangres
derramadas en la arena,
y los toros de Guisando,
casi muerte y casi piedra,
mugieron como dos siglos
hartos de pisar la tierra.
No.
¡Que no quiero verla!

Por las gradas sube Ignacio
con toda su muerte a cuestas.
Buscaba el amanecer,
y el amanecer no era.
Busca su perfil seguro,
y el sueño lo desorienta.
Buscaba su hermoso cuerpo
y encontró su sangre abierta.
¡No me digáis que la vea!
No quiero sentir el chorro
cada vez con menos fuerza;
ese chorro que ilumina
los tendidos y se vuelca
sobre la pana y el cuero
de muchedumbre sedienta.
¿Quién me grita que me asome?
¡No me digáis que la vea!

No se cerraron sus ojos
cuando vio los cuernos cerca,
pero las madres terribles

I will not see it!
Remembrance burns.
Call the jasmine
with their little whiteness!

I will not see it!

The cow of the ancient world
passed her sad tongue
over a snout of blood
spilled on sand,
and the bulls of Guisando,*
death almost, stone almost,
bellowed like two centuries
tired of treading earth.
No.
I will not see it!

Ignacio climbs the steps,
his whole death on his back.
He looked for dawn
and dawn was finished.
He seeks his firm profile,
sleep sets it adrift.
He sought his beautiful body
and found his opened blood.
Do not say I have to see it!
I do not want to feel the flow
lose strength with every beat,
The flow which lights
the cheapest seats and spills
on the corduroy and leather
of the thirsting crowd.
Who shouts at me and beckons?
Do not say I have to see it!

His eyes did not close
when he saw the horns close in,
but the wild mothers

levantaron la cabeza.
Y a través de las ganaderías
hubo un aire de voces secretas,
que gritaban a toros celestes
mayorales de pálida niebla.

No hubo príncipe en Sevilla
que comparársele pueda,
ni espada como su espada
ni corazón tan de veras.
Como un río de leones
su maravillosa fuerza,
y como un torso de mármol
su dibujada prudencia.
Aire de Roma andaluza
le doraba la cabeza
donde su risa era un nardo
de sal y de inteligencia.
¡Qué gran torero en la plaza!
¡Qué buen serrano en la sierra!
¡Qué blando con las espigas!
¡Qué duro con las espuelas!
¡Qué tierno con el rocío!
¡Qué deslumbrante en la feria!
¡Qué tremendo con las últimas
banderillas de tiniebla!

Pero ya duerme sin fin.
Ya los musgos y la hierba
abren con dedos seguros
la flor de su calavera.
Y su sangre ya viene cantando:
cantando por marismas y praderas,
resbalando por cuernos ateridos,
vacilando sin alma por la niebla,
tropezando con miles de pezuñas,
como una larga, oscura, triste lengua,
para formar un charco de agonía
junto al Guadalquivir de las estrellas.

raised their heads.
And from the ranches
a stir of secret voices rose
calling out to celestial bulls,
masters of pale mist.

No prince in Seville
could compare with him,
no sword was like his sword,
no heart so true.
His strength was a marvel,
like a river of lions,
his measured bearing
like a marble torso.
An air of Rome in Andalusia
hung gold about his head,
his laugh a spikenard
of intelligence and wit.
What a fighter in the ring!
What a mountain man in the hills!
How gentle with the corn!
How harsh with the spur!
How tender with the dew!
How dazzling at the fair!
How tremendous with the final
banderillas of the dark!

But now he sleeps for ever.
Now mosses and grass
open with sure fingers
the flower of his skull.
Now his blood comes singing,
singing through marsh and meadow,
sliding down rigid horns,
faltering soulless through mist,
stamped by a thousand hooves
like a long dark sad tongue
becoming a pool of agony
by the Guadalquivir of stars.

¡Oh blanco muro de España!
¡Oh negro toro de pena!
¡Oh sangre dura de Ignacio!
¡Oh ruiseñor de sus venas!

No.
¡Que no quiero verla!
Que no hay cáliz que la contenga,
que no hay golondrinas que se la beban,
no hay escarcha de luz que la enfríe,
no hay canto ni diluvio de azucenas,
no hay cristal que la cubra de plata.
No.
¡¡Yo no quiero verla!!

3. Cuerpo presente

La piedra es una frente donde los sueños gimen
sin tener agua curva ni cipreses helados.
La piedra es una espalda para llevar al tiempo
con árboles de lágrimas y cintas y planetas.

Yo he visto lluvias grises correr hacia las olas
levantando sus tiernos brazos acribillados,
para no ser cazadas por la piedra tendida
que desata sus miembros sin empapar la sangre.

Porque la piedra coge simientes y nublados,
esqueletos de alondras y lobos de penumbra;
pero no da sonidos, ni cristales, ni fuego,
sino plazas y plazas y otras plazas sin muros.

Ya está sobre la piedra Ignacio el bien nacido.
Ya se acabó. ¡Qué pasa! ¡Contemplad su figura!
La muerte lo ha cubierto de pálidos azufres
y le ha puesto cabeza de oscuro minotauro.

Ya se acabó. La lluvia penetra por su boca.
El aire como loco deja su pecho hundido,

O white wall of Spain!
Black bull of sorrow!
Ignacio's hardened blood!
O nightingale of his veins!

No.
I will not see it!
There's no chalice can hold it,
no swallow drink it,
no frost of light chill it,
no song nor deluge of lilies,
there's no glass can silver it.
No.
I will not see it!

3. The Body Laid Out

Stone is a forehead where dreams moan,
devoid of curved water, frozen cypress.
Stone is a shoulder to carry time
with trees of tears and ribbons and planets.

I've seen grey rains scud toward the waves
raising tender brittle arms to avoid
the stone laid out in traps,
loosening limbs, refusing blood.

Stone gathers seeds and clouds,
larks' skeletons and twilight wolves,
but gives out no sound, no crystal, no fire,
only bull-rings, bull-rings, more bull-rings without walls.

Now well-born Ignacio lies on stone.
It is finished. What is happening? Look at him.
Death has covered him with pale sulphur
and given him the head of a dark Minotaur.*

It is finished. Rain rinses his mouth.
Frenzied air abandons his sunken chest,

y el Amor, empapado con lágrimas de nieve,
se calienta en la cumbre de las ganaderías.

¿Qué dicen? Un silencio con hedores reposa.
Estamos con un cuerpo presente que se esfuma,
con una forma clara que tuvo ruiseñores
y la vemos llenarse de agujeros sin fondo.

¿Quién arruga el sudario? ¡No es verdad lo que dice!
Aquí no canta nadie, ni llora en el rincón,
ni pica las espuelas, ni espanta la serpiente:
aquí no quiero más que los ojos redondos
para ver ese cuerpo sin posible descanso.

Yo quiero ver aquí los hombres de voz dura.
Los que doman caballos y dominan los ríos:
los hombres que les suena el esqueleto y cantan
con una boca llena de sol y pedernales.

Aquí quiero yo verlos. Delante de la piedra.
Delante de este cuerpo con las riendas quebradas.
Yo quiero que me enseñen dónde está la salida
para este capitán atado por la muerte.

Yo quiero que me enseñen un llanto como un río
que tenga dulces nieblas y profundas orillas,
para llevar el cuerpo de Ignacio y que se pierda
sin escuchar el doble resuello de los toros.

Que se pierda en la plaza redonda de la luna
que finge cuando niña doliente res inmóvil;
que se pierda en la noche sin canto de los peces
y en la maleza blanca del humo congelado.

No quiero que le tapen la cara con pañuelos
para que se acostumbre con la muerte que lleva.
Vete, Ignacio: No sientas el caliente bramido.
Duerme, vuela, reposa: ¡También se muere el mar!

and Love, drenched with tears of snow,
warms itself among the cattle on the heights.

What are they saying? A stinking silence settles.
We are here with a body fading,
a noble form once full of nightingales
we now see filling with bottomless holes.

Who is crumpling the shroud? What he says is not true!
Here no one sings or weeps in corners,
or pricks their spurs, or startles snakes.
Here I want only wide-open eyes
to see this body which can never rest.

I want to see here strong-voiced men,
men who tame horses, subdue rivers,
men whose skeletons sound, who sing
from mouths packed full with sun and flint.

Here is where I want to see them. Before the stone.
Before this broken-reined body.
I want them to show me the way out
for this captain pinioned by death.

I want them to teach me to weep like a river
of soft mists and steep banks to bear away
Ignacio's body, let him go
without the bulls' double snorting in his ears.

Let him disappear into the round bull-ring
of the little-girl moon feigning a pained still beast.
Let him go into the fishes' songless night,
into the white scrub of frozen smoke.

I do not want them to hide his face with handkerchiefs
to get him used to bearing death.
Go now Ignacio. Do not endure the hot bellowing.
Sleep, soar, rest. The sea also dies!

4. Alma ausente

No te conoce el toro ni la higuera,
ni caballos ni hormigas de tu casa.
No te conoce el niño ni la tarde
porque te has muerto para siempre.

No te conoce el lomo de la piedra,
ni el raso negro donde te destrozas.
No te conoce tu recuerdo mudo
porque te has muerto para siempre.

El Otoño vendrá con caracolas,
uva de niebla y montes agrupados,
pero nadie querrá mirar tus ojos
porque te has muerto para siempre.

Porque te has muerto para siempre,
como todos los muertos de la Tierra,
como todos los muertos que se olvidan
en un montón de perros apagados.

No te conoce nadie. No. Pero yo te canto.
Yo canto para luego tu perfil y tu gracia.
La madurez insigne de tu conocimiento.
Tu apetencia de muerte y el gusto de su boca.
La tristeza que tuvo tu valiente alegría.

Tardará mucho tiempo en nacer, si es que nace,
un andaluz tan claro, tan rico de aventura.
Yo canto su elegancia con palabras que gimen
y recuerdo una brisa triste por los olivos.

4. Absent Soul

The bull does not know you, nor the fig,
nor horses, nor the ants of your house.
The child does not know you, nor the afternoon,
because you have died for ever.

The back of the stone slab does not know you,
nor the black satin where you fragment.
Your silent remembrance does not know you
because you have died for ever.

Autumn will return with conches,
misted grapes and clustering hills,
but no one will want to look in your eyes
because you have died for ever.

Because you have died for ever
like all the dead of the Earth,
like all the dead forgotten
on the heaped-up corpses of dogs.

No one knows you. But I sing you,
sing your profile and grace for later.
Your peerless judgement.
Your embracing of death, the taste of its kiss.
The sadness within your courageous joy.

Not soon, perhaps not ever, will there be
so certain an Andalusian, or so daring.
I sing his elegance in a lament of words
and remember a sad breeze among the olives.

From *Sonetos del amor oscuro*

El poeta habla por teléfono con el amor

Tu voz regó la duna de mi pecho
en la dulce cabina de madera.
Por el sur de mis pies fue primavera
y al norte de mi frente flor de helecho.

Pino de luz por el espacio estrecho
cantó sin alborada y sementera
y mi llanto prendió por vez primera
coronas de esperanza por el techo.

Dulce y lejana voz por mí vertida,
dulce y lejana voz por mí gustada,
lejana y dulce voz amortecida,

lejana como oscura corza herida,
dulce como un sollozo en la nevada,
¡lejana y dulce, en tuétano metida!

'¡Ay voz secreta del amor oscuro!'

¡Ay voz secreta del amor oscuro!
¡Ay balido sin lanas! ¡Ay herida!
¡Ay aguja de hiel, camelia hundida!
¡Ay corriente sin mar, ciudad sin muro!

¡Ay noche inmensa de perfil seguro,
montaña celestial de angustia erguida!
¡Ay perro en corazón!, voz perseguida,
silencio sin confin, lirio maduro.

Huye de mí, caliente voz de hielo,
no me quieras perder en la maleza
donde sin fruto gimen carne y cielo.

From *Sonnets of Dark Love*

The Poet Speaks to his Love on the Telephone

In its sweet housing of wood
your voice watered the sand-dune of my heart.
To the south of my feet it was Spring,
north of my brow bracken in flower.

Down tight space a pine tree of light
sang without dawn or seedbed.
and for the first time my lament
strung crowns of hope across the roof.

Sweet distant voice poured for me.
Sweet distant voice savoured by me.
Sweet distant voice, dying away.

Distant as a dark wounded doe.
Sweet as a sob in snow.
Sweet and distant, in the very marrow!

'*Ay*, Secret Voice of Dark Love'

Ay, secret voice of dark love,
fleeceless bleating—wound!
Needle of bitterness, fallen camellia,
current without sea, city without walls!

Immense night of firm profile,
celestial mountain tall with anguish!
Dog in the heart, hounded voice,
silence unbounded, full-blown lily!

Leave me, hot voice of ice,
don't let me lose my way in the scrub,
among the laments of barren flesh and sky.

Deja el duro marfil de mi cabeza,
apiádate de mí, ¡rompe mi duelo!,
¡que soy amor, que soy naturaleza!

El amor duerme en el pecho del poeta

Tú nunca entenderás lo que te quiero,
porque duermes en mí y estás dormido.
Yo te oculto llorando, perseguido
por una voz de penetrante acero.

Norma que agita igual carne y lucero
traspasa ya mi pecho dolorido,
y las turbias palabras han mordido
las alas de tu espíritu severo.

Grupo de gente salta en los jardines
esperando tu cuerpo y mi agonía
en caballos de luz y verdes crines.

Pero sigue durmiendo, vida mía.
¡Oye mi sangre rota en los violines!
¡Mira que nos acechan todavía!

Noche del amor insomne

Noche arriba los dos, con luna llena,
yo me puse a llorar y tú reías.
Tu desdén era un dios, las quejas mías
momentos y palomas en cadena.

Noche abajo los dos. Cristal de pena
llorabas tú por hondas lejanías.
Mi dolor era un grupo de agonías
sobre tu débil corazón de arena.

Spare my head's hard ivory,
stop my pain, have mercy!
For I am love, I am nature!

The Lover Asleep on the Poet's Breast

You'll never understand how much I love you
because you sleep and are asleep in me.
In tears I conceal you, pursued
by a voice of penetrating steel.

Rule that prods flesh and morning star alike
now pierces my pained breast
and the wings of your stern soul
have been gored by troubled words.

In the gardens waiting people leap
expecting your body and my pain
on horses of light with green manes.

But, my life, sleep on.
Hear my ruined blood in the violins!
They follow us, biding their time!

Night of Sleepless Love

The night above. We two. Full moon.
I started to weep, you laughed.
Your scorn was a god, my laments
moments and doves in a chain.

The night below. We two. Crystal of pain.
You wept over great distances.
My ache was a clutch of agonies
over your sickly heart of sand.

La aurora nos unió sobre la cama,
las bocas puestas sobre el chorro helado
de una sangre sin fin que se derrama.

Y el sol entró por el balcón cerrado
y el coral de la vida abrió su rama
sobre mi corazón amortajado.

Dawn married us on the bed,
our mouths to the frozen spout
of unstaunched blood.

The sun came through the shuttered balcony
and the coral of life opened its branches
over my shrouded heart.

EXPLANATORY NOTES

Book of Poems

First published in Madrid in 1921 by Gabriel García Maroto. The printer was a friend of Lorca's and the costs of the edition were met by the poet's father. According to the dates supplied for each of the poems they were written between April 1918 and December 1920, although they do not appear in chronological order in the text.

Autumn Song

5 *Babel*: according to Genesis, after the Flood, men spoke a single language and lived on the plain of Senaar in Babylon. Moved by the desire for power they planned to construct a city with a tower that would reach Heaven, but God punished them for such an arrogant enterprise by confusing their language so that they could not understand each other. The city was never completed and took the name of Babel.

Minor Song

The images of the nightingale and the fountain are common in the turn of the century brand of poetry cultivated in Spain and Latin America known as *modernismo*.

7 *Cyrano*: a character in a neo-Romantic comedy by Edmond Rostand (1868–1918), loosely based on the life of the French soldier, poet, and philosopher Savinien Cyrano de Bergerac (1619–55). He was in love with his cousin Roxanne but believed himself to be too ugly to court her, mainly on account of his enormous nose.

Don Quixote: the eponymous hero of a novel by Miguel de Cervantes (1547–1616) whose reason was overcome as a result of reading novels of chivalry.

Sad Ballad

This poem is largely constructed from fragments of phrases from children's songs and games from all over Spain. The details are exhaustively detailed in Ian Gibson, 'Lorca's *Balada triste*: Children's Songs and the Theme of Sexual Disharmony in *Libro de Poemas*', *Bulletin of Hispanic Studies*, 46 (1969), 21–38.

11 *Pegasus*: a mythical winged horse, the son of Poseidon and Medusa.

Elegy

13 *Dionysian*: in ancient Greece, Dionysus was the god of vegetation, fertility, wine, intoxication, and even frenzy, music, and drama. He was worshipped by women in rites of an orgiastic nature, which included tearing an animal to pieces.

13 *Ceres*: ancient Roman goddess of the earth. She protected the fertility of crops and the dead.

15 *Black swan*: the swan is another common image in *modernista* poetry.

Inés: Christian virgin and martyr whose cult was very popular in Rome. Commonly represented with a lamb, an allusion to her purity and her name (*agnus* = lamb).

Cecilia: one of the most venerated martyrs in the early Roman Church. She is frequently represented as playing the organ, and is the patron saint of music.

Clara (1193/4–1253): inspired by the teaching of St Francis of Assisi this saint gave up all her possessions and founded a religious order known as the Poor Clares.

Spring Song

In this poem, as in the earlier 'Minor Song', the theme of nostalgia for a lost childhood is implicit in the way in which the poet ruefully notes his distance from the children mentioned in the poems.

Ballad of the Little Square

The idea of the separation of the poet from the experience of childhood, present in 'Spring Song' and 'Minor Song', is given a more dramatic rendering in this poem on account of its dialogue form.

The Billy Goat

35 *Don Juan*: a legendary profligate who has been interpreted down the centuries as the epitome of the seducer. One of the earliest literary manifestations of this figure was Don Juan Tenorio in *El burlador de Sevilla* (*The Trickster of Seville*) by the seventeenth-century Spanish playwright Tirso de Molina (1584?–1648).

Mephistophelian: Mephistopheles was a familiar spirit of the devil in later settings of the legend of Faust.

Pan: in Greek mythology, a fertility deity more or less bestial in form. Pan was generally regarded as vigorous and lustful, having the horns, legs, and ears of a goat.

37 *Philommedes*: mentioned in Hesiod's *Theogany*, Philommedes is an alternative name for Aphrodite, and connotes 'lover of genitals'. She is supposed to have been born from Uranus' genitals, which had been hacked off and thrown into the sea.

Anacreon: Greek poet of the sixth century BC. Famous for his epigrams and erotic poetry, he was renowned as a pleasure-seeker.

Suites

Lorca conceived the idea of writing groups of poems as suites towards the end of 1920 when he was composing the final poems of *Libro de poemas*. He worked assiduously on his *Suites* until 1923, frequently mentioning their forthcoming publication in letters. The intention was to publish them as part of a threefold project that was also to include *Poema del cante jondo* and *Canciones*. Yet only a handful of the suites appeared in Lorca's lifetime; it was in 1983 that a version reconstructed by André Belamich was published (Madrid: Ariel).

Sesame

41 *Narcissus*: in Greek mythology, a handsome youth who was so obsessed with his own beauty that he was oblivious of the love of the nymph Echo. He became enamoured with his own image reflected in the waters of a well, and died of anguish because he could not reach it. He was transformed into a flower of the same name.

In the Garden of Lunar Grapefruit

47 *Don Carlos the Pretender*: Carlos Luis de Borbón (1818–61) was given the mantle of Carlist pretender by his father, Don Carlos, Conde de Molina, in 1845. He made two unsuccessful attempts to seize the Spanish throne.

Poem of the Cante Jondo

Conceived in the summer of 1921, the bulk of the poems that make up this collection were written in November of the same year, coinciding with Lorca's interest in flamenco and his involvement in the preparations for the *cante jondo* festival in Granada in the following summer. It was not until May 1931 that the book was finally published (Madrid: Ulises), with the addition of some new material.

Dancing the Siguiriya

A phonetic deformation of *seguidilla*, *siguiriya* is one of the basic forms of *cante jondo*.

The Soleá

Soleá: a contraction of *soledad* (solitude). Together with the *siguiriya* it comprises the most profound of the *cante jondo* forms, and is characterized by passionate lament.

Bowmen

67 *Guadalquivir*: the name given by the Arabs to the river known to the Romans as Betis. One of the largest rivers in Spain, it flows into the Atlantic Ocean beyond Seville.

Procession

71 *Merlins*: Merlin was a legendary magician and wise man, attached to the court of King Arthur.

Ecce Homo: literally 'Behold the man'—an exhortation to contemplate Christ on the Cross.

71 *Durandarte*: a character in Spanish versions of French Carolingian romances. It was originally the name that Roland gave to his sword. There is an allusion to Durandarte in the episode of Montesinos's cave in Don Quixote.

73 *Orlando furioso*: the eponymous hero of an epic poem by Ariosto, who was driven mad by amatory jealousy. He is also mentioned in *Don Quixote*.

Saeta

See Introduction, p. xv.

73 *See where he comes!*: a phrase found in many traditional *saetas*, alluding to the appearance of Christ bearing the Cross.

Songs

It is probable that Lorca did not contemplate writing a book to be entitled *Canciones* until 1926, though the bulk of the ninety poems that comprise this collection had been written by that date. Indeed, in one of his letters Lorca suggests that seventy of these poems were written between 1921 and 1923, but even if that were to be strictly true, the poems were subjected to careful revision in the following years, while the tasks of organization and ordering were only undertaken shortly before the eventual publication date of May 1927 (Malaga: Litoral).

Nocturnes at the Window

The structure of the opening section of this poem with its binary formulations is typical of many poems in *Songs*. See D. Gareth Walters, *Canciones and the Early Poetry of Lorca: A Study in Critical Methodology and Poetic Maturity* (Cardiff: University of Wales Press, 2002), 25–30.

Verlaine

The subject of this poem is the French poet Verlaine (1844–96) whose liaison with the poet Arthur Rimbaud was a source of scandal.

Bacchus

The subject of this poem is the Latin god Bacchus (another name for Dionysus; see note to 'Elegy' above).

Juan Ramón Jiménez

The subject of this poem is the Spanish poet Jiménez (1881–1956) whose work is informed by the aesthetic ideal.

Venus

The subject of this poem is Venus, the Roman goddess of love, originally a goddess of the Spring who protected vines and gardens, and later identified with the Greek goddess Aphrodite.

Debussy

The subject of this poem is the French composer Debussy (1862–1918) whose work is regarded as the musical equivalent of Impressionism. Several compositions of his were inspired by the movement of water.

Narcissus

The subject of this poem is Narcissus, the youth discussed in the note to 'Sesame' above.

The Moon Appears

The moon is perhaps Lorca's commonest image and symbol, variously suggestive of mystery, fate, and death.

Light Madrigal

The diminutive form of 'madrigal' in the Spanish text ('Madrigalillo') suggests an element of mockery or even parody.

Gypsy Ballads

As with *Canciones* the poems that appear in *Romacero gitano* cover several years. The earliest was written at the end of 1921 but the majority of the eighteen poems that make up the collection were written much later: ten ballads were published individually between 1926 and 1928 prior to the publication of the first edition in July 1928 (Madrid: Revista de Occidente).

Ballad of the Moon, the Moon

107 *forge . . . anvil*: gypsies were commonly associated with the trade in horses, hence the allusions to the forge and anvil.

   barn-owl: a portent of death in Andalusia as elsewhere.

Dreamwalker Ballad

113 *Civil Guards*: a rural paramilitary police force founded in 1842, and the traditional enemy of the Gypsies. They were accustomed to patrolling in pairs.

The Gypsy Nun

115 *five wounds of Christ*: the making of crystallized fruit was a common occupation of nuns in Andalusia and many of these sweets bore such religious names.

Dead from Love

123 *St George*: the patron saint of soldiers. Here the allusion is to the fury he displayed in his legendary slaying of the dragon.

125 *azure telegrams*: telegrams were printed on blue paper in Spain.

Poet in New York

Written during the period Lorca spent in New York in 1929–30, the poems were published posthumously, appearing in two differing editions in successive months in 1940 (New York: Norton; Mexico City: Seneca). These editions vary in their canon, text, and order, and there is no consensus as to which better represents the poet's final intentions. In 1932 Lorca prepared a lecture-recital of poems from the collection, but continued to change his mind about the organization of the collection.

Cry to Rome

137 *the man dressed in white*: an allusion to Pope Pius XI. See Introduction, p. xxi.

Blacks in Cuba, Their Son

The *Son* is a Cuban song of African origin.

141 *Fonseca . . . Romeo and Juliet*: references to the names and illustrations on the covers of cigar boxes.

Earth and Moon

In mid-1933 Lorca was working towards a collection entitled *Tierra y Luna*, including poems written as much as four years earlier and coinciding with his period in New York. *Little Infinite Poem* bears the date of 10 January 1930.

The Tamarit Divan

Lorca started work on this collection in the summer of 1931 but most of the poems were written in the spring and summer of 1934. The book was initially destined for publication by the University of Granada, Lorca's home university, but for reasons that are unknown the edition never appeared. With the outbreak of the Spanish Civil War in 1936 the project was abandoned, and the work eventually appeared in a special issue of *Revista Hispánica Moderna* (New York, 1940). The term 'Divan' comes from the Persian *diwan*, meaning 'collection' or 'anthology'. Lorca is less precise, however, about the use of the two terms employed as titles for the poems in this collection, and evidently uses the words in a purely evocative fashion The qasida refers to a fairly long poem with a single rhyme, while the ghazal is a short poem of between four and fifteen lines, normally of an erotic nature.

Ghazal of the Morning Marketplace

151 *Elvira's Arch*: the gate that leads into the Gypsy, formerly the Moorish, quarter of the Albaicín in Granada.

Six Galician Poems

The poems that make up this tiny collection were written between 1932 and 1934, Lorca having visited Galicia three times in the earlier of these years. It was published in Santiago de Compostela at the end of 1935 (Editorial Nós).

Cradle Song for Rosalía de Castro, Dead

155 *Santiago*: Santiago de Compostela, the capital of Galicia, and renowned as a place of pilgrimage because the bones of the Apostle James were supposedly found there.

Lament for Ignacio Sánchez Mejías

Lorca's poetic response to the death of Mejías (see Introduction, p. xxii) was immediate. The poem was completed within three months of the bullfighter's death in August 1934, and published in Madrid (Cruz y Raya: Ediciones del Árbol) in the March or April of the following year.

157 *the bull alone elated*: a phrase that uncannily anticipates a dominant detail of Picasso's *Guernica*, painted in response to the bombing of the Basque town of that name during the Spanish Civil War.

161 *the bulls of Guisando*: an allusion to Iberian sculptures near Avila of four animals presumed to be bulls, and possibly associated with an ancient cult of the animal.

165 *Minotaur*: in Greek mythology a creature, half-bull, half-man, that guarded the labyrinth at Minos.

Sonnets of Dark Love

These poems were written mainly in the autumn of 1935. The surviving texts are first drafts; it seems likely that later versions have been lost. Many of the eleven poems that make up the cycle remained unpublished until December 1983 when they were printed, probably in Madrid, by the bibliophile Victor Infantes in an anonymous limited edition unauthorized by the poet's family.

INDEX OF TITLES

After Passing By 53
Aire de nocturno 16
Al oído de una muchacha 88
Alba 64
amor duerme en el pecho del poeta, El 172
And After 55
Another Song 31
Another Way 103
Arqueros 66
Autumn Song 3
¡Ay! 58
Ay! 59
Bacchus 85
Baco 84
Balada de la placeta 22
balada del agua del mar, La 26
Balada triste 8
Balcón 72
Balcony 73
Ballad of the Little Square 23
Ballad of the Moon, the Moon 107
Betrothal 97
Billy Goat, The 33
Blacks in Cuba, their *Son* 141
Bowmen 67
Canción bajo lágrimas 40
Canción con reflejo 38
Canción de jinete 80
Canción de noviembre y abril 102
Canción del naranjo seco 104
Canción menor 6
Canción otoñal 2
Canción primaveral 18
Canción tonta 80
Canzón de cuna pra Rosalía Castro, morta 152
Capture of Antoñito el Camborio on the Seville Road 117
Casida V Del sueño al aire libre 146
Casida VIII De la muchacha dorada 148
Cave 63
Cradle Song for Rosalía Castro, Dead 153
Crossroads 59
Crucifixion 133

Crucifixión	132
Cry to Rome	137
Cueva	62
Dagger	57
Dancing the *Siguiriya*	53
Dawn ('But like love's/arrows . . .')	73
Dawn ('Córdoba bells/at daybreak . . .')	65
De otro modo	102
Dead from Love	123
Death of Antoñito el Camborio	119
Debussy	86, 87
Delirio	44
Delirium	45
Despedida	98
Desposorio	96
Después de pasar	52
Dream ('I rode astride . . .')	29
Dream ('My heart rests beside . . .')	21
Dreamwalker Ballad	109
Elegía	12
Elegy	13
En el instituto y en la universidad	98
En el jardín de las toronjas de luna	44
Encrucijada	58
Encuentro	64
¡Es verdad!	82
First Anniversary	93
Fishermen	43
Float, Holy Week	71
Foolish Song	81
Gacela del Mercado matutino	150
Gacela IX Del amor maravilloso	146
Ghazal IX Of Marvellous Love	147
Ghazal of the Morning Marketplace	151
Grito hacia Roma	136
grito, El	50
Guitar, The	49
guitarra, La	48
Gypsy Nun, The	113
He Died at Dawn	91
Horizon	43
Horizonte	42
Horseman's Song	81
In a Girl's Ear	89
In the Garden of Lunar Grapefruit	45
In the Institute and in the University	99
It's true!	83
Juan Ramón Jiménez	84, 85

King of Harlem, The 127
Lament for Ignacio Sánchez Mejías 157
Landscape 49
Landscape without Song 43
Light Madrigal 101
Little Infinite Poem 145
Llanto por Ignacio Sánchez Mejías 156
Lover Asleep on the Poet's Breast, The 173
Lucía Martínez 94, 95
luna asoma, La 90
macho cabrío, El 32
Madrigalillo 100
Madrugada 72
Malaise and Night 95
Malestar y noche 94
Meeting 65
Minor Song 7
monja gitana, La 112
Moon Appears, The 91
Muerte de Antoñito el Camborio 118
Muerto de amor 122
Murió al amanecer 90
Narciso 88
Narcissus 89
Night 67
Night of Sleepless Love 173
Noche 66
Noche del amor insomne 172
Nocturnal Air 17
Nocturnes at the Window 77
Nocturnos de la ventana 76
Otra canción 30
Paisaje 48
Paisaje sin canción 42
Parched Land 55
Parting 99
Paso 70
paso de la Siguiriya, El 52
Pequeño poema infinito 144
Pescadores 42
Poet Speaks to his Love on the Telephone, The 171
poeta habla por teléfono con el amor, El 170
Prelude 101
Preludio 100
Prendimiento de Antoñito el Camborio en el camino de Sevilla 116
Primer aniversario 92
Procesión 70
Procession 71

Pueblo	56
Puñal	56
Qasida V Of the Open-Air Dream	147
Qasida VIII Of the Golden Girl	149
rey de Harlem, El	126
Romance de la luna, luna	106
Romance of Our Lady of the Boat	153
Romance sonámbulo	108
Romaxe de Nosa Señora da Barca	152
Sad Ballad	9
Saeta	70
Saeta	71
Seawater Ballad	27
Second Anniversary	93
Segundo aniversario	92
Sesame	41
Sésamo	40
Sevilla	68
Seville	69
Shout, The	51
Silence, The	53
silencio, El	52
Soleá, La	60
Soleá, The	61
soltera en misa, La	94
Son de negros en Cuba	140
Song beneath Tears	41
Song of November and April	103
Song of the Dry Orange Tree	105
Song with Reflection	39
Sorpresa	60
Spinster at Mass, The	95
Spring Song	19
Sueño ('Iba yo montado sobre . . .')	28
Sueño ('Mi corazón reposa junto . . .')	20
Surprise	61
Tierra seca	54
Town	57
Venus	86, 87
Verlaine	82, 83
Y después	54

INDEX OF FIRST LINES

A Calvary	57
A las cinco de la tarde	156
A sun without rays	43
Abejaruco	94
Alta va la luna	76
Among black butterflies	53
Antonio Torres Heredia	116, 117
Apples with flesh-wounds	137
As soon as there's a full moon, I'll go to Santiago, Cuba	141
Así te vi	86
At five in the afternoon	157
¡Ay qué trabajo me cuesta	82
¡Ay ruada, ruada, ruada	152
¡Ay voz secreta del amor oscuro!	170
Ay, secret voice of dark love	171
Bajo el moisés del incienso	94
Bee-eater	95
Beneath the cradle of incense	95
Blue sky	43
But like love's	73
Campanas de Córdoba	64
Cantan los niños	22
Child!	89
Cielo azul	42
Cirio, candil	66
Como un incensario lleno de deseos	12
Con todo el yeso	146
Con una cuchara	126
Córdoba	80, 81
Córdoba bells	65
Cristo Moreno	70
Cuando llegue la luna llena iré a Santiago de Cuba	140
Cuando sale la luna	90
Cuatro granados	100
Dark Christ	71
De la cueva salen	62
Dewdrops	7
Disuelta la tarde	44
Down alleyways	71
Dressed in black cloaks	61
East wind	59
El árbol gigantesco	42
El campo	48

El cielo nublado   102
El grito deja en el viento   58
El mar   26
El puñal   56
El rebaño de cabras ha pasado   32
El reflejo   40
¡El sueño se deshizo para siempre!   30
Empieza el llanto   48
En aquel sitio   40
En el blanco infinito   84
En la pradera bailaba   38
Entre mariposas negras   52
Equivocar el camino   144
¡*Érguete, miña amiga*   152
Flor de jazmín y toro degollado   146
Four pomegranate trees   101
Fragmented evening   45
From the cave   63
Green how I want you green   109
Green murmur, intact   85
Happy children emerge   19
He lay in the street, dead   61
Hoy siento en el corazón   2
I didn't want to   89
I rode astride   29
I saw you thus   87
I'm petrified   17
I've said goodbye to the friends . . .   45
Iba yo montado sobre   28
If I die   99
In its sweet housing of wood   171
In that place   41
In the end the moon could stay on the horses'
    blinding white curve   133
In the infinite white   85
In the meadow   39
In the still night   23
Jasmine bloom and butchered bull   147
La canción   82
La elipse de un grito   50
La hoguera pone al campo de la tarde   102
La Lola   72
La luna clava en el mar   92
La luna pudo detenerse al fin por la curva blanquísima
    de los caballos   132
La luna vino a la fragua   106
La muchacha dorada   148
La niña va por mi frente   92

La primera vez	98
Lamp, candle	67
Las alamedas se van	100
Leñador	104
Like a censer filled with desires	13
Lola	73
Los arqueros oscuros	66
Los laberintos	54
Los niños miran	52
Lucía Martínez	94, 95
Mamá	80
Mama	81
Manazanas levemente heridas	136
Me he despedido de los amigos . . .	44
¡Mi corazón es una mariposa	8
Mi corazón reposa junto a la fuente fría	20
Mi sombra va silenciosa	86
Muerto se quedó en la calle	60
My child, hear the silence	53
My heart rests beside the cool fountain	21
My heart's a butterfly	9
My shadow moves silently	87
Ni tú ni yo estamos	64
Night of four moons	91
Niño	88
No quise	88
Noche arriba los dos, con luna llena	172
Noche de cuatro lunas	90
On the evening land the bonfire lays	103
Oye, hijo mío, el silencio	52
Parched land	55
Pero como el amor	72
Pilgrimage, pilgrimage!	153
Por el arco de Elvira	150
Por la calleja vienen	70
—¿Qué es aquello que reluce	122
Rise, sweet friend	153
Salen los niños alegres	18
Sevilla es una torre	68
Seville is a tower	69
Si muero	98
Silence of myrtle and lime	113
Silencio de cal y mirto	112
Sobre el monte pelado	56
Sobre la verde bruma	42
Tengo mucho miedo	16
The avenues of poplar go	101
The children watch	53

The cloudy sky   103
The dagger   57
The dark bowmen   67
The dream came apart for good!   31
The field   49
The first time   99
The giant tree's lianas   43
The girl passes across my brow   93
The golden girl   149
The guitar begins   49
The herd of goats passed where   33
The labyrinths   55
The moon came to the forge   107
The moon nails to the sea   93
The moon rides high   77
The night above. We two. Full moon   173
The reflection is   41
The sea   27
The shout   51
The shout leaves a cypress shadow   59
The song   83
Through Elvira's Arch   151
Throw this ring   97
Tienen gotas de rocío   6
Tierra seca   54
Tirad ese anillo   96
To take the wrong road   145
Today in my heart   3
Tú nunca entenderás lo que te quiero   172
Tu voz regó la duna de mi pecho   170
Verde que te quiero verde   108
Verde rumor intacto   84
Vestida con mantos negros   60
Viento del Este   58
Virgen con miriñaque   70
Virgin with crinoline   71
Voces de muerte sonaron   118
Voices of death sounded   119
'What is that gleaming   123
What it costs me   83
When the moon rises   91
With a spoon   127
With all the gypsum   147
Woodsman   105
You and I   65
You'll never understand how much I love you   173

A SELECTION OF   **OXFORD WORLD'S CLASSICS**

LUDOVICO ARIOSTO   **Orlando Furioso**

GIOVANNI BOCCACCIO   **The Decameron**

LUÍS VAZ DE CAMÕES   **The Lusiads**

MIGUEL DE CERVANTES   **Don Quixote de la Mancha**
                         Exemplary Stories

CARLO COLLODI   **The Adventures of Pinocchio**

DANTE ALIGHIERI   **The Divine Comedy**
                         Vita Nuova

LOPE DE VEGA   **Three Major Plays**

J. W. VON GOETHE   **Faust: Part One and Part Two**

LEONARDO DA VINCI   **Selections from the Notebooks**

FEDERICO GARCIA LORCA   **Four Major Plays**

NICCOLÒ MACHIAVELLI   **Discourses on Livy**
                         The Prince

MICHELANGELO   **Life, Letters, and Poetry**

PETRARCH   **Selections from the Canzoniere and**
                         Other Works

GIORGIO VASARI   **The Lives of the Artists**

HONORÉ DE BALZAC	**Père Goriot**
CHARLES BAUDELAIRE	**The Flowers of Evil**
DENIS DIDEROT	**Jacques the Fatalist**
	The Nun
ALEXANDRE DUMAS (PÈRE)	**The Count of Monte Cristo**
	The Three Musketeers
GUSTAVE FLAUBERT	**Madame Bovary**
VICTOR HUGO	**The Essential Victor Hugo**
	Notre-Dame de Paris
J.-K. HUYSMANS	**Against Nature**
PIERRE CHODERLOS DE LACLOS	**Les Liaisons dangereuses**
GUY DE MAUPASSANT	**Bel-Ami**
	Pierre et Jean
MOLIÈRE	**Don Juan and Other Plays**
	The Misanthrope, Tartuffe, and Other Plays
ABBÉ PRÉVOST	**Manon Lescaut**
ARTHUR RIMBAUD	**Collected Poems**
EDMOND ROSTAND	**Cyrano de Bergerac**
JEAN-JACQUES ROUSSEAU	**Confessions**
MARQUIS DE SADE	**The Crimes of Love**
STENDHAL	**The Red and the Black**
	The Charterhouse of Parma
PAUL VERLAINE	**Selected Poems**
VOLTAIRE	**Candide and Other Stories**
ÉMILE ZOLA	**L'Assommoir**
	The Kill